A Study into Financial Globalization, Economic Growth and (In)Equality

Fikret Čaušević

A Study into Financial Globalization, Economic Growth and (In)Equality

palgrave
macmillan

Fikret Čaušević
School of Economics and Business
University of Sarajevo
Sarajevo, Bosnia and Herzegovina

ISBN 978-3-319-51402-4 ISBN 978-3-319-51403-1 (eBook)
DOI 10.1007/978-3-319-51403-1

Library of Congress Control Number: 2017933079

Printed on acid-free paper

This Palgrave Macmillan imprint is published by Springer Nature
The registered company is Springer International Publishing AG
The registered company address is: Gewerbestrasse 11, 6330 Cham, Switzerland

Contents

List of Figures

List of Tables

CHAPTER 1

Introduction

The thesis that financial liberalization is essentially beneficial for economic growth, particularly under conditions of increased globalization of financial markets and trade, was first put forward systematically in a number of articles in the early 1970s. Their starting point was the assumption that financial liberalization and globalization would produce more efficient financial markets, because private financial institutions necessarily outperform state- or publicly owned ones, channelling resources more effectively towards projects with longer-term sustainability and higher rates of return and so fostering economic prosperity. This thesis has never been without its detractors and seems to fit the facts at best only imperfectly. The main purpose of this book is to test it.

To take just the most glaring example, China has been one of the five fastest-growing economies in the world for each of the last twenty-five years. In 1978, Deng Xiaoping started the opening-up to international flows of goods, services, and capital and by the beginning of the current decade what had been one of the world's poorest countries was its second largest economy.[1] As a result, the most populous country in the world is now also one of its most important capital markets, with a share in world market capitalization up from just 1% in 2000 to more than 15% in early 2015. In the 2014–2015, there were four Chinese

This book has been edited by a native English speaker, Desmond Maurer, MA, to whom I express my special thanks.

F. Čaušević, *A Study into Financial Globalization, Economic Growth and (In)Equality*, DOI 10.1007/978-3-319-51403-1_1

banks among the ten largest in the world. Their combined assets were 2% greater than Chinese gross domestic product (GDP) in 2015.[2]

These are undoubtedly impressive results. It was not, however, based upon a radical turn towards financial liberalization. As late as 2015, the economy was still relatively financially closed by International Monetary Fund (IMF) criteria. Most restrictions on *short-term* capital flows were still in place, as was majority state ownership of the banking sector, although the Chinese authorities allowed for a mixed ownership in those banks by mayor western banking groups since 1999. Indeed, the authorities only deregulated the financial market, scrapping the deposit interest rate ceiling, in October 2015, perhaps their most important move towards financial liberalization for two years.

On the other hand, World Bank data for the 1981–2014 show $2,583 billion of net foreign direct investment (FDI), making the Chinese economy one of the de facto most open. If China was the world's largest exporter of goods by the beginning of the 2010s, therefore, it was thanks largely to legal changes that had opened it up to capital investment, particularly in export-oriented projects. China's exceptional economic performance has not been due to the relative closure or openness of its economy, but to the particular balance struck between the two. The example of China makes clear the need for a critical review of the financial liberalization hypothesis.

In Chapter 2, we review the early work in the field from the 1960s and early 1970s, followed by a more detailed critique of key academic works from the past twenty years. In the following three chapters, we look at financial liberalization and globalization's combined impact on economic growth and inequality around the world over the past twenty-five years, but more particularly during the first fourteen years of this century. The example of China might, after all, conceivably be an outlier, however massive, and a systematic evaluation of the hypothesis of the impact of financial liberalization and globalization on growth can only be done on *a cross-country basis.* These three chapters therefore comprise a comparison of the economic performance of all countries for which data for 1990 through 2014 is available from the World Bank database.

To facilitate this, we have introduced a simple but informative new measure of relative economic standing, which we call the growth coefficient. It is the ratio of a country's share in world GDP to its share in world population, using data on GDP and population from the World Bank database. The comparison of national growth coefficients for 1990 to 2014 allows us to note at least three significant results immediately.

First is the fairly clear absence of strict correlation between quickly adopted measures of de jure financial liberalization and faster economic growth, in developing countries at least. This is clear from the example of the countries of the Far East and South-East Asia. When they laid the groundwork of their financial successes, they did so with only gradual financial opening-up. They applied financial liberalization measures as part of broader macroeconomic policies aimed at creating high economic growth rates and improving relative economic standing through export-led growth. Capital account openness went together with strategic incentives to FDI, as a key source of capital for export-oriented investment strategies. This approach allowed them to maintain net positive international investment positions and become net exporters of capital (especially China).

Second is that financial liberalization and globalization over the past twenty-five years has involved major paradox. The United States and the United Kingdom, the two most financially sophisticated countries in the world, are both net importers of capital. Both they and the other countries of Western Europe and Scandinavia (the EU 15) saw increasing financial flows over the first fourteen years of this century, but they were negatively correlated to their relative economic standing. In the periods 2000–2008 and 2009–2014, approximately three-quarters of internationally active banks' claims related to the most-developed countries, which were essentially lending to each other.[3] This did not stop their growth rates lagging significantly behind the world average. Some, like Italy and Greece, even experienced very significant reductions in both absolute GDP per capita and their growth coefficients. The falling coefficients make quite clear the negative correlation in developed countries between growing financial flows and falling relative economic standing, in the fourteen years to 2015. This suggests flows were less about investment in manufacturing than financial transactions on the interbank and derivatives markets. It also confirms Maurice Obstfeld and Alan Taylor's observations from 2002 about the key role taken on financial markets by diversification finances during the second financial globalization (which began during the 1970s and continues today).

The third is that a high degree of positive correlation does seem to exist between rapid financial liberalization and major improvement in relative economic standing in the case of the countries in transition (Central Europe, the Baltic, South-eastern Europe, and at least part of Eastern Europe) during the 2000s. Opening up their banking sectors to FDI was a key element of liberalizing their financial systems at the turn of the century. As a result, their banking sectors are largely owned by Western European banks. Credit flows from money-centre countries proved a key channel for creating liquidity, deposit multiplication, and the fast growth of credit activity in these countries and was a key element in speeding up their rates of growth. Financial and trade liberalization went hand in hand. Between 2001 and 2014, ten of the twenty fastest-growing economies in the world were transition countries. Another eight were developing countries and just two were developed economies. The non-oil-exporting countries relied primarily on domestic-demand-induced growth. As a result, most of them faced sharply rising current account deficits. This is an important feature of how financial liberalization and economic growth interact. It means that the really pressing questions are those related to liberalization's impact on and the sustainability of rapid economic growth, given growth's dependence on the quality of the economic policy being applied, under the various institutional and political arrangements.

The global crisis in 2008 helped bring to light a number of scandals and abuses on financial markets in which major private financial groups, including JP Morgan Chase&Co, Barclays, Royal Bank of Scotland, the Deutsche Bank, and UBS, played key roles. Fiddling the Libor, fixing exchange rates, and abusing derivatives' markets to get around the Basel II capital adequacy ratio requirement were just some of the ways fully liberalized financial markets were being abused in the most-developed countries. Such events have helped further undermine the financial liberalization thesis.

The focus in the final chapter is on particular problems and paradoxes of financial globalization, its relationship to economic growth, and the policy measures taken over the last six years by highly developed countries in attempts to tackle the global economic crisis. The chapter closes with a review of recent proposals by financial experts to tackle these issues and of the author's own proposal for how financial markets in transition and developing countries might be broadened and deepened through a network of guarantee schemes to underwrite issues of safe assets.

Notes

1. Measured in GDP expressed in absolute US dollars.
2. This impressive banking sector growth is somewhat reminiscent of the Japanese banking sector's dominance during the 1980s: in 1981 only one of the ten largest banks in the world was Japanese; by 1988, nine were; today, none are.
3. According to the data provided by the Bank for International Settlements for the relevant periods.

CHAPTER 2

Financial Globalization and Economic Growth – Literature Review with Comments

2.1 Seminal Works on Financial Structures and Liberalization

Theoretical discussion of how financial systems and financial liberalization affect economic growth started in the 1960s and 1970s with works by such authors as William Goldsmith,[1] Edward Shaw[2] and Ronald McKinnon.[3] For William Goldsmith, the basic point was that financial structures are an integral aspect of market economies and so play a very important role in enabling higher growth rates: More developed financial systems foster faster economic growth.

Edward Shaw and Ronald McKinnon argued that financial liberalization's impact on economic growth would be positive. They distinguished between financially repressed and financially liberalized economies and identified the difference as lying in deregulation, the removal of interest rates ceilings, the liberalization of both short and long-term capital flows, and the elimination of state interference in bank decision-making over which sectors to lend to and at what terms. They held that withdrawal of the state from interest rate regulation and the public ownership of banks and consequently higher interest rates on deposits would allow financial systems to attain higher savings levels. Higher savings would mean more investment and more efficient lending to higher-return sectors. From a macroeconomic perspective, they expected this to foster higher growth rates and more rational use of savings over the longer term.

F. Čaušević, *A Study into Financial Globalization, Economic Growth and (In)Equality*, DOI 10.1007/978-3-319-51403-1_2

The proponents of financial liberalization also argued that removing obstacles to international capital flows, by opening-up their financial systems rapidly towards relatively capital-rich countries (with high levels of savings), would mean savings were deployed much more productively, as investing in countries with poorer access to capital and labour would yield higher returns, as well as making capital-poor developing countries more attractive to capital inflows. Financial liberalization would thus be a win-win game: The owners of capital in developed countries receive higher returns on capital abroad, while income from labour in the newly opened-up developing countries is rising, thanks to the improving capital/labour ratio and higher wages.[4]

The next major theoretical advance was due to Hyman Minsky, who developed his financial instability hypothesis in a number of publications through the 1970s and 1980s,[5] arguing, against mainstream economics, that financial systems should not be considered a neutral sector in macro-economic models. Far from just transferring savings to borrowers, managers of financial institutions have an autonomous incentive as managers to innovate in financial products and financial institutions. The financial sector is a creator of deposits thanks to its ability to create them through the banks' core business – extending credit. In periods of take-off, expanding credit becomes an endogenous creator of new deposits. Innovation by financial institutions means speculative and Ponzi-style institutions play an ever-increasing role in the structure of highly developed economies, thanks particularly to the intensive use of financial leverage. This promotes both financial instability and the instability of the developed economies more generally. Contrary to standard equilibrium-based models of supply and demand for financial resources, developed economies therefore need Big Government because of their inherent tendency towards instability.[6]

2.2 Financial Globalization and Its Effects

In early 2002, Maurice Obstfeld and Alan Taylor published their study on financial globalization's impact on economic growth.[7] They compared the structural arrangements for international capital flows and impact on economic growth for the First (1870–1914) and Second Financial Globalizations (1970–2000). Their main points were:

- During the first financial globalization, international capital tended to flow from rich to poor countries. Nearly three quarters of these flows were pro-development.

- Under the second financial globalization, financial flows were considerably more likely to be between rich countries, with "diversification" financing winning out over development financing.
- This diversification financing was due to rapid expansion in financial innovation and financial derivatives whose main purpose was to protect powerful players on global financial markets against risk (interest rate risk, foreign currency risk, credit risk).

In the years after Obstfeld and Taylor published their study, the pattern of capital flows largely supported their findings. Between 2002 and 2008, transactions on derivative markets and lending by internationally active banks expanded sharply, creating an appearance of liquidity growth on international financial markets, but this apparent liquidity was utilized, at least in part, for regulatory arbitrage and to get around international banking standards.

In 2006, Kose, Prasad, Rogoff, and Wei[8] published an article looking at financial openness' impact in developing countries over the thirty-year period ending in 2003/2004. In part six of their article, they look at the structure of long-term capital flows and its impact on economic growth. Based on the sources and data available to them, they found no clear evidence that FDI *necessarily* contributes to economic growth or even the avoidance of economic crisis. They did however find significant evidence portfolio investment has positive effects on economic growth and argued that a major distinction has to be made between de jure and de facto financial openness.

Indeed, that a high rating for de jure financial openness is not necessary to ensure a significant impact on economic growth has since become a commonplace of studies on this topic.[9] Some of the fastest-growing economies in the world (e.g. China and the countries of South-east Asia) have had high levels of de facto financial globalization, in spite of being classified as de jure relatively closed economies. The results of our investigations into the relative economic standing of developed and developing countries and changes in the pattern over time, presented in the next chapter and based on the World Bank database, make clear that, during the first fourteen years of this century, fewer than half of the 20 fastest-growing economies had implemented full de jure financial openness.[10]

They argued that any analysis of financial globalization's impact would therefore have to pay proper attention to institutional stability and the approaches taken to reform. In contrast to the classical framework their approach stresses financial globalization's collateral effects and their importance for how the traditional channels of influence (financial markets and institutions) function. This in turn determines the impact of financial flows, better management, and macroeconomic discipline. How these elements interact affects total factor productivity (TFP) growth and so GDP growth, allowing changes in the public's consumption and wealth to take place smoothly.

In an essay from 2006, Gourinchas and Jeanne[11] deploy a calibrated neoclassical model of economic growth to argue against the standard interpretation of financial openness and its impact on a typical capital-recipient developing country. They found that for a typical non-OECD country, the conventionally measured impact on growth and prosperity of transition from financial autarky (financial repression) to full financial liberalization is no more than 1% of steady domestic consumption growth. They consider this gain negligible compared to the productivity-based increases in prosperity in the countries from their sample which did not pursue full financial liberalization.

Rodrik and Subramanian are also critical of financial globalization's supposed benefits for economic growth.[12] In their critical review of the literature, they conclude that financial globalization has not in fact been a key factor in countries recording faster economic growth. In Chapter 12 of their book *Economic Growth*,[13] Robert Barro and Xavier Sala-i-Martin present the results of a regression analysis of the impact of explanatory variables on economic growth, namely that the "state of financial development" is not a key variable, but one of the additional explanatory variables, and that the development of financial markets is endogenous, an integral part, and logical consequence of economic growth itself.

These findings are of signal importance for macroeconomic modelling and for the different views assumed by the post-Keynesians, on the one hand, and the New Classical and New Keynesian macroeconomists, on the other. These theoretical differences in starting point and their greater or lesser deviation from the realities of developed capitalism are enormously significant for any potential application to real-world economic policy-making and its capacity for counter-cyclical effectiveness.

In *Stabilizing an Unstable Economy*,[14] Hyman Minsky sets out the key reasons the neoclassical synthesis cannot provide a consistent answer to the problem of the business cycle.[15] He argues that the causal links between investment and the financial system mean any analysis of the investment process must take into account the development of financial institutions in capitalist societies. In earlier periods, banking served primarily to finance trade, but modern industrial capitalism is characterized by a far greater need for money and financial instruments to support investment in fixed capital, without which no development of industrial capitalism would have been possible.

Minsky further explained his financial instability hypothesis in a paper from 1992,[16] arguing that, in developed-market economies, entrepreneurship plays a major role and financial industry managers have an endogenous incentive to develop and innovate financial products related to the process of financing the real sector. Their profit motives and financial product development are therefore primarily endogenous in character and should be approached as a special factor in the process of economic growth. Development of the financial system gives speculative and Ponzi-like financial institutions an ever-greater role in its own development and in that of the economy as a whole. This growing importance of financial leverage in financing the purchase of financial assets and property necessarily promotes instability of the system.

The structure and development of IMF country-members' financial systems since the early 1970s have meant that financial innovations have been generated almost exclusively in the developed economies or the international financial institutions (e.g. the interest rate swaps introduced by the World Bank in the early 1970s). Innovation has proceeded in lockstep with the growing complexity of the real sector and growing needs for investment financing. This has resulted in partial confirmation of Minsky's financial instability hypothesis for *developed economies*, where financial-market sophistication is primarily endogenously determined and managers in financial institutions enjoy inherent incentives to innovate in financial products and augment profits, in line with expansion of the sector overall, but not for small open and larger developing countries with underdeveloped networks and structures of economic institutions, where financial openness is an exogenous variable to the local economic system. Exogenous here refers to the fact that, under the second financial globalization, small open economies lacked the endogenous capacity to innovate in financial products and create liquidity growth themselves. Growth in liquidity or lending was therefore primarily a function of financial liberalization and integration of the local financial systems (esp. the major banks) into the financial systems of the money-centre countries whose banks used FDI to buy up the local financial sector, so that liquidity and lending growth on the local markets were exogenously determined by the endogenously determined financial innovations in financial systems of the foreign investing countries.

In a 1999 paper, Barry Johnston, Salim Darbar, and Claudia Echeverria examine the sequencing of capital account liberalization in four emerging-market countries.[17] They explain the nature of capital account liberalization and the events that led to the Asian Currency Crisis (the crisis of 1997/1998), demonstrating that the currency crisis was preceded by a sizeable build-up of short-term foreign liabilities. The authors single out five implications of the crisis for capital account liberalization: the sustainability of inflows depends on how efficiently funds are used; adequate risk management incentives are critically important for a country's ability to avoid excessive direct external borrowing by non-bank corporations; increased reliance on short-term borrowing can be an indicator of uncertainty about future economic growth and its sustainability; speeding-up the development of longer-term security markets through domestic capital-market reforms and by removing capital controls can be useful and desirable; and once the crisis had begun, reintroducing controls helped in the cases of Thailand, Indonesia, and Korea.[18]

2.3 Deregulation versus Regulation

In a 2003 article, Jean Tirole presented an analysis of the "micro-bases" for taking on debt to finance new investments.[19] His basic aim was to explore the economic justification, if any, for capital control measures. In his answer, he deployed a combination of micro- and macroapproaches, finding that ramping up external debt is not necessarily a bad decision from a macroperspective, if additional debt is used for investments that increase the income of the company's owners or shareholders. In line with agency theory, so long as additional debt and the investment it finances increase net cash flows and shareholder wealth, thanks to increased net profits in the corporate sector, any such increase in debt will be internalized with positive externalities, increasing wealth at household level. If, however, debt-financed new investment reduces returns on equity, additional debt will drag down liquidity and solvency at the microlevel and heighten the risk of insolvency at the macro-level. In the latter case, introducing capital controls is fully justified.

In an article from 2011, in which he offers a good review of the literature on the economic rationale for introducing capital controls under conditions of financial amplification and pecuniary externalities,[20] Anton Korinek argues that prudential capital controls are justified during phases of the business cycle when aggressive borrowing (sharp increases in financial leverage) leads domestic financial players to take on additional risks. This imposes negative monetary externalities on society as a whole, reduces the overall level of prosperity or wealth, and increases financial instability.

In a book published in 2012,[21] Jeanne, Subramanian, and Williamson offer their analysis whether controls for international capital flows are ever desirable and, if so, when and how to introduce them. In their view, good reasons exist for introducing certain types of capital controls, particularly prudential controls and counter-cyclical measures to control capital flows, which are largely directed towards damping down cyclical deviations in the economy – whether in the boom or the bust phase of the business cycle. This is because the global economic system lacks a common set of rules regarding international capital flows, in contrast to the rules established for international trade in goods and services. According to the authors, IMF members should agree a framework, but whether or not to apply controls should be left up to individual member-countries. Capital control measures should be introduced to reduce the impact of speculative capital on major fluctuations in financial asset prices, but they should be market-based rather than administrative measures, with a special emphasis on price-based capital control measures. Capital transactions should be taxed at up to 15%,[22] the level their calibrated model suggests as the optimum tax rate on speculative capital flows.

2.4 Measuring Financial Openness: De Jure and De Facto Measures

In the literature on financial liberalization and globalization, measures of financial openness tend to be categorized into two main groups. The first is de jure measures, which are based on the methodology and systematization developed after the IMF Annual Report on Exchange Arrangements and Exchange Restrictions (AREAER). The second is de facto measures, itself classified into two subgroups. The first is based on price differentials, which can be measured using either the uncovered or the covered interest rate parity. For the latter, there must be a forward market and forward interest rates. The second subgroup of de facto measures of financial openness is based on international price arbitrage. In the following text, we will review a number of the indices that have been developed over the past couple of decades.

The standard index for de jure openness is that developed by Menzie Chinn and Hiro Ito and called by them the KAOPEN or capital account openness index.[23] In addition to de jure measures of capital account openness, the fully worked out version also integrates the following variables: the presence of multiple exchange rates, the presence of restrictions on current account transactions, indicating restrictions on capital account transactions, and indicating a requirement to surrender export proceeds.

In their analysis of the quality and information content of the various indicators of financial openness,[24] Quinn, Schindler, and Toyoda single out the Chinn-Ito KAOPEN and the Brune and Guisinger FOI (financial openness index) as the most comprehensive de jure measures, covering the longest periods.[25] The KAOPEN is publicly available, however, while the FOI is not. As a result, the KAOPEN is the more extensively used and the one we shall rely on in our analyses.[26] In their overall review, Quinn, Schindler, and Toyoda organize the indicators into three categories: de jure, de facto, and hybrid indicators.[27] They consider TOTAL (the ratio of the sum of a country's total assets and liabilities to GDP) the index of choice in de facto measures of financial openness, as it is the broadest, covering all flows in both directions.

In two papers from 2006 and 2014,[28] Philip Lane and Gian Maria Milesi-Ferretti present their index of de facto financial openness and findings based on it. Their index comprises the ratio of the sum of data on financial flows (FDI, portfolio investment, bank and trading loans, financial derivatives, and reserve assets other than gold) in both directions (assets plus liabilities) to GDP and allows comparison of de jure and de facto financial openness.

The authors' analyses concur with that in Chapter 3 below in suggesting that countries with relatively low indices for de jure openness may nonetheless attract and absorb significant amounts of capital. China, one of the fastest-growing economies in the world, is a good example. Its Chinn-Ito index remained very low for many years (1980–2014), regardless of the fact that it was a world leader in terms of net FDI inflows over the first fourteen years of this century (total net FDI to China for 2000–2014 was $2,259 billion according to the World Bank database).

Ranciere, Tornell, and Westermann consider an economy de facto financially liberalized if the capital-inflows-to-GDP ratio in or prior to a given year (t) was at least 10% *or* at least 5% and the country had just ceased being a financially closed economy. Capital inflows here are considered to include the sum of FDI, portfolio flows, and bank flows.[29] They conducted a regression analysis on data for 60 countries for the period 1980–2002, demonstrating that financial liberalization may have had a positive impact on economic growth, but that it has also contributed to the phenomenon of recurrent recession and financial crisis. They conclude that, for the period they were looking at, the gains from financial liberalization outweighed the costs in GDP lost or foregone during periods of recession, not least thanks to the availability of capital.

In an article from 2003,[30] Graciela Kaminsky and Sergio Schmukler present their indicator of financial openness based on the degree of financial liberalization in three sectors: the capital account, the domestic financial sector, and the stock market. They applied it separately to each sector and as a composite index for partial or full financial liberalization, with a range from one to three, from complete financial liberalization (1) to financial repression (3).[31] The authors claim their analysis proves financial liberalization did cause increased financial instability over the short term in the countries they studied, but that developing countries have also experienced benefits from financial liberalization over the longer term, as reflected in accelerated rates of economic growth thanks to capital flows from developed countries, while its impact in developed countries that have adopted the full range of financial liberalization measures over both the short and long run has been faster growth and other economic benefits.

The Kamisky-Schmukler study drew upon data covering the 1973–1998. This was the period, particularly from the early 1980s, when financial liberalization was becoming a major element of economic programs adopted in the most-developed countries, especially the United States and the United Kingdom. Financial innovations promoted after full liberalization on their highly sophisticated financial markets were a key factor in deepening and broadening those markets, as well as in their impact on other major financial actors around the world, in particular through repeal of the famous Glass-Steagall Act in 1999 and signing of the Commodity Futures Modernization Act in December 2000 by Bill Clinton at the end of his second term.

Together with the adoption of consultative papers, and of CP-2 (2001) in particular, these regulatory changes in the United States allowed the megabanks to calculate their required capital to risk-weighted assets ratios on the basis of internal ratings, even before Basel II (2004). This helped open up space for financial institutions to enjoy full financial freedom and carry out financial transactions on derivative markets de facto either without or with at best extremely superficial external controls, as well as take advantage of financial innovations for regulatory arbitrage. Data from the Bank for International Settlements (BIS) show an increase in the notional amounts outstanding on OTC-traded derivatives contracts from $95.2 trillion in December 2000 to $683.7 trillion in June 2008.[32] According to the same source, lending by globally active banks was increasing at twice the rate between 2002 and 2008 that it had between 1985 and 2002.[33] This was what led to the greatest financial crisis since the Great Depression being generated in the most-developed economies and it being in precisely those economies that financial liberalization and innovation on derivative markets produced the greatest financial shocks and an unprecedented increase in financial volatility.

In Chapter 3, below, we look at changes in relative economic standing for all the countries for which the World Bank has published GDP figures.[34] Our analysis shows that most of the 20 fastest-growing economies between 2000 and 2014 were either developing (including countries in transition) or undeveloped countries. We find that financial globalization and trade liberalization were indeed key factors for accelerated economic growth during the first fourteen years of this century in transition countries. The other subgroup (Azerbaijan, Kazakhstan, and Equatorial Guinea) owes its faster growth largely to rising energy prices, their main source of income. Even in those countries, however, FDI into the oil industry was the most important factor contributing to increased oil production and so rising export income.

Financial liberalization's positive impact on economic growth was particularly characteristic of transition countries from Central, South-eastern, and Baltic Europe during the first decade of this century. Financial integration through FDI in the banking sector had an immediate spill-over effect through changes to lending and knock-on further changes to the (C+I+G) component of GDP creation. This spill-over channel functioned in both directions: so long as credit operations or lending in Western Europe were on the rise (between 2000 and 2008), so was lending in Central, South-eastern, and Baltic Europe, at above average rates, with a consequent direct impact on economic growth. Economic growth in almost all these countries, however, was predominantly based on domestic demand-led growth and they have all faced sharply increased current account deficits since as a result.

As credit activity in Western Europe fell sharply, the spill-over channel brought about a sharp decrease in lending in Central, South-eastern, and Baltic Europe, resulting in economic decline or at best modest growth rates in most of the countries involved (with the exception of Baltic Europe). So at least in the case of transition countries from Central and South-east Europe, contrary to the Kaminsky-Schmukler findings for the 1973–1998 period for developing countries, quickly adopted measures of de jure financial openness that were followed by a sharp increase in de facto openness in the 1995–2005 had had a positive impact on economic growth in the short-to-medium term, which has been followed by a major financial instability in the longer term.

The Rodrik-Subramanian paper points out that, over the long run (two or three decades), sustainable economic growth depends on investment and that the problem of sustainable growth in developing countries has been less about lack of savings than lack of investment, especially in building a good base for producing tradable goods. Tradable goods require more investment than non-tradables, as investing in the manufacturing base requires simultaneous reforms (and investment) in institution building and steps to support export-led growth.[35] They also stress the need to distinguish between desirable FDI and other types of financial flows (portfolio and credit flows), as the former is related largely to increasing the productive base, the latter often to increases in financial inflows that cause appreciation of the domestic currency and reduce the competitiveness of developing countries facing a sudden increase in capital flows.

In his 2006 book,[36] Mishkin presented his arguments for financial globalization's importance for economic growth in developing and emerging markets. In chapter eight, "Ending Financial Repression: The Role of Globalization", he points out that developing institutional infrastructure is key to the success of financial globalization, and it entails: developing property rights, strengthening the legal system, reducing corruption, improving the quality of financial information, improving corporate governance, and getting the government out of the business of directing credit.[37] Other factors Mishkin stresses include: the importance of prudential regulation and supervision based on limiting currency mismatches, the proper role of deposit insurance, restricting connected lending, ensuring that banks have plenty of capital, focusing on risk management, and encouraging disclosure and market-based discipline.[38]

All these factors are of undoubted significance for financial globalization's success in effecting sustainable economic growth. Mishkin, however, focuses primarily on developing- and emerging-market economies and their financial systems. The global crisis of 2008 showed that the primary source of major financial shock was in fact megabanks based in the United States, United Kingdom, and Western Europe. A major paradox of the crisis, which is in essence still ongoing, is that it manifested in democratic and institutionally highly developed environments – the leading economies of the world. The crisis generated in these highly developed economies spilled over to the financial systems of developing and emerging-market economies, and especially to those that had already undertaken rapid financial liberalization. Whichever of Mishkin's six factors one takes as key to successful prudential regulation and supervision, the US, UK, and EU financial systems all failed. Their leading financial institutions faced very serious problems of maturity mismatches, connected lending, very bad risk management, and too "tiny" a capital base.

In a paper from 2015, Bush deploys an econometric model to examine the relationship between de jure and de facto financial openness.[39] His analysis of de jure openness's impact on de facto openness and so of legal liberalization on gross capital flows reveals a positive causal relationship for the top decile (the developed group of countries), which does not however hold for the lowest decile in his sample. He shows an average value of de jure openness from 1980 to 2011 of 2.62, with a minimum of 0.38. For the top decile (the most-developed countries), each unit increase in de jure openness induces an increase of 0.39 in gross capital stocks.[40] For countries below the median for de jure openness, there appears to be a negative relationship between increases in de jure openness and gross capital flows.

2.5 Uneven Economic Growth, Adapting Economic Policies in Low-Income Countries, and Some Potential Solutions

In their 2014 book,[41] Peter Temin and David Vines explain why the economic recovery has been so slow: recession in EU countries is due to the most-developed economies' trade surplus, as the low real Euro exchange rate has boosted their ability to export at the expense of the Southern Eurozone, whose real exchange rate is higher, rendering them uncompetitive, and causing a constant need for them to import savings. They also stress that for most countries with a balance of payment adjustment problem (generally small open economies) faster economic recovery depends on the major economies, China, Germany, the United Kingdom, and the United States, changing their economic policies. The solution they propose is based on Keynes's recommendations for countercyclical action. The economies with major international reserves or a major capacity for taking on public debt and so conducting an expansionary fiscal policy should stimulate domestic demand, while simultaneously reducing export surpluses (first and foremost Germany and China), and increasing demand for imported goods from small open economies, which cannot attain economic growth on the grounds of domestic demand alone.[42]

Economic policy coordination between developed and fast-growing developing countries, and more particularly medium-to-lower-income countries with small open economies, is inadequate not least because of the dominant mindset in macroeconomic theory, with reliance on its models from the New Classical and New Keynesian economics. These schools differ considerably in their assumptions, but agree in relying on rational expectations and models developed with the advanced countries and the coordination of their economic policies in mind. The Obstfeld-Rogoff *Redux* model is an example, as it incorporates rational expectations within an explicitly worked-out microeconomic basis for the maximization of household utility and corporate profits. This model was developed to apply to a pair of large developed high-income economies with similar household preferences and involved in intensive horizontal intra-industry trade combined with inter-industry trade. The model's strength lay in providing a clear New Keynesian answer to the New Classical macroeconomics' objection that, Keynesian models lacked a clearly specified and firm microeconomic basis. The *Redux* model of an open economy does not, however, serve well the analysis of changes under the sort of equilibrium/disequilibrium conditions in the global economy which have, over the past two decades, increasingly conditioned trade between developed countries and the fast-growing large developing economies.

These dominant macroeconomic models rely on all the relevant information being available to all market participants and on well-functioning institutions. As such they hardly represent a sound basis for economic policy in countries faced with insufficiently developed institutional systems, insufficient access to information, and correspondingly significant market imperfections. It is nonetheless possible to adapt the economic models of a world of highly competitive markets to the world of largely imperfect markets, particularly by taking into account the fairly high barriers to entry. Such models can then be of significant use to economic policy in emerging, developing, and less-developed countries. Dani Rodrik explains how useful such alternative economic models can be for economic policy, so long as economists confront the way markets really work.[43]

In a 2008 article,[44] Quinn and Toyoda use a sample of 94 countries to investigate capital account liberalization's impact on economic growth between 1950 and 2004. The model is a five-year, non-overlapping model with lagged variables, using the previous five-year average for the explanatory variables as values influencing the change in GDP for the following five-year period. As well as an initial version of their model, based on OLS, the authors also developed an alternative based on the General Methods of Moments (GMM), to allow explanatory variables to be endogenous. Their test measures change in GDP based on changes in the following explanatory variables: income, investment, population, trade volume, revolutions and coups, oil prices, and capital flows.[45] The authors used the capital and fin-capital de jure measures of capital account and current account openness as their measures of financial openness. Their analysis confirmed a strong and robust relationship for both developed and developing countries between financial openness (based on the de jure measures) and economic growth.

Given the analytical period (from 1958 to 2004 in the GMM model) and their use of the impact of explanatory variables from a preceding five-year period on a dependent variable in the subsequent five-year period, they were clearly not in a position to analyze changes during the first fourteen years of the current century. Their final data set was an annual average for the explanatory variables from 1994 to 1999, allowing them to look at its impact on GDP for the five-year period from 2000 to 2004. To apply their approach to the first fourteen years of this century would require an analysis of the impact of changes in the explanatory variables for the period from 2001 to 2005 on economic growth in 2006 to 2010 and then of changes in that period on economic growth from 2011 to 2015. The results of our own analysis of changes in relative economic standing (Chapter 3 below) indicate that the G-10 countries all experienced negative rates of change in their growth coefficient (the ratio of their shares in world GDP and in world population). These are all countries that had carried out full financial liberalization before 2000. Average concentration of banks' liabilities in them ranged between 85 and 90%, as measured by the geographical distribution of internationally active banks' liabilities.[46]

In other words, the intensification of financial flows between financial institutions and within the group of developed countries from 2005 to

2009 had no positive impact on GDP growth and in the 2000–2014 led to no improvement in these countries' *relative economic standing*. Their per capita GDP growth rates fell relative to the global per capita growth rate by anything from 0.5% (Sweden) to 23.4% (Italy).[47] This suggests that, particularly in the developed countries and in the significantly more integrated global financial environment of the first fourteen years of the current century, financial liberalization and globalization's impact on economic growth has shifted the burden of interbank lending to financing speculative transactions and away from financing the manufacturing sector' productive base (productivity growth).

Few of the papers reviewed in this chapter consider the structure of financial flows in terms of the distinction between diversification finance and developmental finance, Obstfeld-Taylor and Rodrik-Subramanian being the exceptions. The first years of the century saw international banks engage in very intense lobbying for the Basel II banking rules and new models for determining ratings and risk. Even before Basel II was finalized (June 2004), under Consultative Paper 2,[48] most international banks could already apply internal models for determining ratings and risk weightings based on them. As CP 2 was agreed in 2001, international banks were therefore already maintaining low capital/asset and capital/RWA ratios. They ramped up lending over 2002 to 2008. In practice, asset quality review, supposed to be one of the bases for early warning, was very superficially implemented. The steep growth in leverage in the banking sector meant few banks in the major developed countries would be in a position to compensate for the losses that appeared in the meantime because of conflicts between their trading and risk management departments. The key to analyzing financial openness and liberalization's impact on economic growth in developed countries therefore lies in the highly dysfunctional system of prudential controls and oversight over the major financial institutions and their operations. The largest banking groups in the developed countries were effectively out of control.

2.6 Some Observations on the Adjustment Process Before and After the Crisis

In a paper from 2014,[49] Lane and Milesi-Ferretti examine global imbalances and external adjustment in 64 developed and emerging-market countries. A regression analysis comparing current account balances for the 2005–2008 and 2008–2012 revealed that most of the sample ran above average current account deficits (the average was calculated using fitted values). Those with above average deficits during the boom phase (2005–2008) were, however, better able to improve them afterwards. Comparing data for a two-year and a four-year sub-period, 2008–2010 and 2008–2012, they examined the link between credit activity and the current account balance and found a very high correlation between the 2008–2010 change in the current account and the 2008–2012 change, concluding that improvement in it could not be attributed solely to disruption in the credit markets during the trough of the business cycle (the 2008 crisis).[50]

Their conclusion fails to take into account fully the problems at least in core-European countries' banking sectors (the mother banks' home countries) or changes in the major Eurozone banks' credit activity and the structure of the assets side of their balance sheets. These banks' major problems emerged in 2010–2012 (and have continued to do so since, but their paper does not cover the period after 2012). The sovereign debt crises in EU and especially Eurozone countries and institutional changes, bailout measures, and new banking rules and practices have led to very cautious credit procedures, causing stagnation and even a decline in lending by the major banking groups in the Eurozone.

The process of restructuring and cleaning the major banks' balance sheets is ongoing in the Eurozone, United Kingdom, and even United States, as a result of the new requirements imposed by the Basel Committee for Banking Supervision (Basel III), the Dodd-Frank Act (in the United States), and new ECB and EBA rules on banking supervision in the Eurozone, including implementation of the Bank Recovery and Resolution Directive (BRRD) aimed at preventing the costs of potential future banking crises being borne by Eurozone taxpayers rather than the shareholders and creditors/ depositors of the major banks and deposit-taking institutions. In other words, the rise in uncertainty after the 2008–2009 crisis in the banking industry around the world (the most important countries financial centres) and especially in the Eurozone has resulted in a very modest expansion in lending to households and a modest decline in lending to business, inducing a fall in the (C+I) segment of GDP creation and forcing those countries to repair their current account balances between 2008 and 2012 (and since) as a countercyclical measure, along with an unprecedented increase in the G segment of GDP creation, based on fast-growing public indebtedness (with the exception of Germany).

Data from the ECB's Report on Financial Structures[51] reveal the unprecedented change in the banking sector assets in the leading countries of Western Europe since the onset of the global crisis. Even in the three countries running current account deficits between 2004 and 2012 (France, Spain, Italy), where banking assets saw positive change between 2009 and 2012, this increase was not associated with any increase in lending to businesses, but rather with increased holdings of government bonds (lending to government) in the first place. The leading factor in credit expansion during the boom (2004–2008) was lending to companies. This increase in lending to companies was running nearly 60% ahead of the increase in lending to households. The bust period, followed by a period of slow recovery, was characterized by declining credit activity to businesses – the single most important segment of credit activity as an indicator of the potential for job creation in the business sector. Between 2004 and 2008, lending to non-financial corporations was up EUR1.665 trillion, only to decline by EUR274 million over the following four years (2008–2012). Lending to households by the Eurozone banking sector was up EUR1.088 trillion during the boom (2004–2008). Over the next four years, it increased by only about one-third of the increase it had experienced during the boom.[52]

Such widespread pessimism on the part of entrepreneurs in Eurozone business sectors is hardly exceptional – similar business sentiment has been recorded in other parts of the developed world. Lending to governments was a leading component in Eurozone credit activity between 2008 and 2014. This period in Eurozone banking sector management practices has been characterized as a flight to quality (to "a safe haven", i.e. government bonds).

Notes

1. Goldsmith 1969; Goldsmith 1959.
2. Shaw 1973.
3. McKinnon 1973
4. This standard (neo)classical way of thinking about the benefits of financial openness was challenged by Robert Lucas in a paper from 1990, in which he introduced the so-called Lucas Paradox. Lucas 1990.
5. Minsky 2008 (1986).
6. Minsky 2008, pp. 330–343.
7. Obstfeld and Taylor 2002.

8. Ayhan Kose, Eswar Prasad, Kenneth Rogoff, and Shang-Jin Wei, 2006.
9. See e.g. Klein 2009. This book offers a particularly good and comprehensive literature review and commentary on financial globalization's impact on economic growth.
10. See Chapter 3 below.
11. Gourinchas and Jeanne 2006.
12. Rodrik and Subramanian 2009.
13. Barro and Sala-i-Martin 2001.
14. Minsky 2008.
15. Minsky 2008, pp. 111–112.
16. Minsky 1992.
17. Johnston, Darbar, and Echeverria in Johnston and Sundararajan eds., 1999.
18. Johnston, Darbar, and Echeverria 1999.
19. Jean Tirole 2003.
20. Korinek 2011.
21. Jeanne, Subramanian, and Williamson 2012.
22. Jeanne, et al. 2012, p. 113.
23. Quinn, Schindler, Toyoda 2011, p. 491.
24. Quinn, et al. 2011.
25. Their de jure category includes (i) indicators based on the AREAER Categorical Table of Restrictions, (ii) indicators based on the text of AREAER, and (iii) non-AREAER de jure indicators.
26. Chinn and Ito 2008.
27. Quinn, et al. 2011, pp. 515–516. Overall, they look at the relevance and importance of the following measures of financial openness: CAPITAL (a de jure measure with a range from 0 to 100), eGlobe-KOF (a blended de facto/de jure measure with a range from 20 to 99), EQUITY (a de jure binary – 0/1- measure), FIN-CURRENT (a de jure measure with a range from 0 to 100), FORU (a blended de facto measure), KA (a de jure measure with a range from 0 to 1), IF-HERITAGE (a de jure measure), Inward FDI (a de facto measure expressed in % GDP), and TOTAL (a de facto measure – the ratio of the sum of a country's total assets and liabilities to its GDP).
28. Lane and Milesi-Ferretti 2006. Idem 2014.
29. Ranciere, Tornell, and Westermann 2006, p. 20.
30. Kaminsky and Schmukler 2003.
31. Kaminsky and Schmukler 2003, Appendix: Figure 1 "Index of Financial Liberalization" and Figure 2 "Indexes of Financial Liberalization by Sector".
32. Source BIS. Data for 2000 are available on the website – http://www.bis.org/publ/otc_hy0105.pdf; data for 2008 are taken from: http://www.bis.org/publ/otc_hy0905.pdf.
33. BIS 2010, pp. 6–7.
34. See Chapter 3 below and tables in the Appendix.

35. Rodrik and Subramanian 2009, pp. 131–134.
36. Mishkin 2006.
37. Mishkin 2006 pp. 130–31.
38. Mishkin 2006 pp. 137–43.
39. Bush 2015.
40. Bush 2015, p. 21.
41. Temin and Vines 2014.
42. Temin and Vines, 2014, p. 105.
43. Rodrik 2015, p. 164.
44. Quinn and Toyoda 2008.
45. Quinn and Toyoda 2008, p. 1419.
46. See: BIS Banking Statistics – available at: http://www.bis.org/statistics/a4_1.pdf
47. The author's calculations based on the World Bank database.
48. Secretariat of the Basel Committee on Banking Supervision 2001, available at: http://www.bis.org/publ/bcbsca01.pdf.
49. Lane and Milesi-Ferretti 2014.
50. Lane and Milesi-Ferretti 2014, p. 10.
51. European Central Bank 2015.
52. European Central Bank 2015, p. 60.

References

Bank for International Settlements. (2010). *Long-term issues in international banking* (CGFS Papers No. 41) Basel (July).

Barro, R. J., & Sala-i-Martin, X. (2001). *Economic growth.* Cambridge, MA, London, England: The MIT Press.

Bush, G. (2015). Capital flows – De Jure vs. De Facto financial openness. *Social Science Research Network* (November), http://papers.ssrn.com/sol3/papers.cfm?abstract_id=2688584

Chinn, M. D., & Ito, H. (2008, September). A new measure of financial openness. *Journal of Comparative Policy Analysis, 10*(3), 309–322.

European Central Bank. (2015, October). *Report on financial structures.* Frankfurt am Main.

Goldsmith, R. W. (1959). Financial structure and development as a subject for international comparative study. In National Bureau of Economic Research (Ed.), *The Comparative Study of Economic Growth and Structure* (pp. 114–123). Washington, DC: NBER.

Goldsmith, R. W. (1969). *Financial structure and development.* London: Yale University Press.

Gourinchas, P. O., & Jeanne, O. (2006). The elusive gains from international financial integration. *Review of Economic Studies, 73*, 715–741.

Jeanne, O., Subramanian, A., & Williamson, J. (2012). *Who needs to open the capital account.* Washington, DC: Peterson Institute for International Economics.

Johnston, R. B., Darbar, S. M., & Echeverria, C. (1999). Sequencing capital account liberalization: Lessons from Chile, Indonesia, Korea, and Thailand. In R. B. Johnston, & V. Sundararajan (Eds.), *Sequencing financial sector reforms – country experiences and issues* (pp.245–294). Washington, DC: International Monetary Fund. Chapter 6.

Kaminsky, G. L., & Schmukler, S. L. (2003, June). *Short run pain, long run gain: The effects of financial liberalization* (NBER Working Paper Series 9787). Washington, DC: National Bureau of Economic Research.

Klein, W. (2009). *Financial globalization and the crisis of 2008-2009.* Washington, DC: Peterson Institute for International Economics.

Korinek, A. (2011). *The new economics of capital controls imposed for prudential reasons* (IMF Working Paper WP/11/298). Washington, DC.

Kose, A., Prasad, E., Rogoff, K., & Wei, S. J. (2006, August). *Financial globalization: A reappraisal* (Working Paper Series WP/O6/189). Washington, DC: International Monetary Fund.

Lane, P. R., and Milesi-Ferretti, G. M. (2006, March). *The external wealth of nations mark II:Revised and extended estimates of foreign assets and liabilities, 1970–2004* (IMF Working Paper WP 06/69). Washington, DC.

Lane, P. R., and Milesi-Ferretti, G. M. (2014, August). *Global imbalances and external adjustment after the crisis* (IMF Working Paper WP 14/151). Washington, DC.

Lucas, R. E. (1990, May). Why doesn't capital flow from rich to poor countries. *The American Economic Review, 80*(2), 92–96.

McKinnon, R. I. (1973). *Money and capital in economic development.* Washington, DC: The Brookings Institution.

Minsky, H. P. (1992, May). *The financial instability hypothesis* (Working Paper, No. 74). The Jerome Levy Economics Institute of Bard College.

Minsky, H. P. (2008). *Stabilizing an unstable economy.* New York: The McGraw Hill Companies.

Mishkin, F. S. (2006). *The next great globalization.* Princeton: Princeton University Press.

Obstfeld, M., & Taylor, A. (2002). *Globalization and capital markets* (NBER Working Paper, 8846). Washington, DC: National Bureau of Economic Research.

Quinn, D. P., & Toyoda, A. M. (2008). Does capital account liberalization lead to growth. *The Review of Financial Studies, 21*(3), 1403–1449. Oxford University Press.

Quinn, D., Schindler, M., & Toyoda, A. M. (2011). Assessing measures of financial openness and integration. *IMF Economic Review* (International Monetary Fund, Washington, DC), *59*(3), 488–522.

Ranciere, R., Tornell, A., & Westermann, F. (2006). *Decomposing the Effects of Financial Liberalization Effects: Crisis vs. Growth* (NBER Working Paper No. 12806). Washington, DC: National Bureau of Economic Research.

Rodrik, D. (2015). *Economics rules – why economics works, when it fails, and how to tell the difference*. Oxford: Oxford University Press.

Rodrik, D., & Subramanian, A. Why did financial globalization disappoint? *IMF Staff Papers* (International Monetary Fund 2009), *56*(1), 112–138.

Shaw, E. S. (1973). *Financial deepening in economic development*. Oxford: Oxford University Press.

Temin, P., & Vines, D. (2014). *Keynes – useful economics for the World economy*, Cambridge, MA: The MIT Press.

Tirole, J. (2003, December). Inefficient foreign borrowing: A dual- and common-agency perspective. *The American Economic Review*, *93*(5), 1678–1702.

Websites:

BIS: http://www.bis.org/publ/otc_hy0105.pdf

BIS: http://www.bis.org/publ/otc_hy0905.pdf.

BIS Banking Statistics: http://www.bis.org/statistics/a4_1.pdf

CHAPTER 3

Global Economic Growth, Financial Openness, and Inequality: 1990–2014

3.1 A Method for Measuring Relative Economic Growth

The past twenty-five years have seen major changes in the world of global flows in goods, services, and capital. These have in turn affected the relations of global economic and financial power.

- In 1990, Chinese GDP per capita was 12.4 times less than the world average.[1] The figure for the second most populous country in the world, India, was even lower, at 14.3 times less. In other words, both the most populous countries in the world placed among the 30 poorest countries, at least for which data was available in the World Bank database.
- A quarter of a century later, in 2014, China's GDP per capita had increased by a factor of 8.3. By 2010, it had become the second largest economy and the largest exporter of goods in the world. Indian GDP per capita had not grown at quite such an impressive rate, but was nonetheless 3.1 times greater in 2014 than in 1990.

Searching for a way to measure and represent such changes in economic power and the relative economic standing of all the countries in the world in my earlier work, *Economic Sovereignty and Global Capital Flows*, I developed what I term the growth coefficient (Cg).[2] This coefficient is

F. Čaušević, *A Study into Financial Globalization, Economic Growth and (In)Equality*, DOI 10.1007/978-3-319-51403-1_3

Table 3.1 Examples of how to calculate the growth coefficient (Cg) for 2000

Country	*GDP in 2000 in millions of 2005 constant USD*	*Population in 2000*	*Share of country in World GDP (in %)*	*Share of country in World population (in %)*	*Growth coefficient (Cg) for 2000*
China	1,423.92	1,262.65	3.524363855	20.77430133	0.170
Denmark	247.447	5.34	0.612461602	0.087859033	6.971
Egypt	75.404	66.137	0.186634126	1.088152226	0.172
Estonia	9.922	1.397	0.024558164	0.022984844	1.068
Finland	179.907	5.176	0.445291838	0.085160741	5.229
France	2,030.04	60.911	5.024597395	1.002168835	5.014

Source: Calculated by the author using World Bank data on GDP and population.

simple, representing the ratio of a country's share in world GDP to its share in world population, or (Table 3.1):

Cg = (Country's GDP/World GDP)/(Country's population/World population)

While a country's rank in terms of the value of this coefficient corresponds to its ranking on the basis of absolute GDP per capita, the "information" contained allows the analyst direct insight into how its GDP per capita stakes up against the world average (the world average is a benchmark):

- A coefficient of 2.255 means a country's GDP per capita is 2.255 times world average GDP per capita (or 225.5% of world GDP per capita).
- A coefficient of 0.333 or, indeed, 0.033 for a given year informs the reader directly that that country's GDP per capita is 33.3% and 3.3% of world GDP per capita, respectively.

As the coefficient presents relative change in economic performance (changes in a country's GDP per capita growth rate relative to change in the world average GDP per capita growth rate), one can calculate the average change in a country's Cg by dividing the factor of its GDP per capita growth by the factor of average world GDP growth, where by factor we mean the sum of unity and the percentage change in GDP per capita (added if a rise, subtracted if a fall). It is worth noting that the percentage *change* in the Cg will be greater than that in GDP per capita. This is because the Cg measures improvement or worsening *relative* to percentage change in average world GDP.

We give two examples below. One when there is an absolute reduction or fall in a country's GDP per capita and one when it is rising, but at slower rate than the world average rate. World GDP per capita rose nearly 20.1%, in 2005 constant US$, between 2000 and 2014 and this is the figure we use in both examples. This means the factor of growth of average world GDP for that period was 1+0.201, or 1.201.

- In the first case, the country's GDP per capita fell 8.05%, so that its factor of growth was 1−0.0805, or 0.9195.The factor for calculating the fall in Cg for the country is thus got as follows: (1−0.0805)/(1+0.201) = 0.9195/1.201 = 0.7656. This represents a fall of 23.4% (1−0.7868 = 0.2344).
- In the second case, the country's GDP per capita was up 7.5% in 2014 on 2000, so that its factor of growth was 1+0.075 or 1.075. Its Cg would therefore have changed as follows: 1.075/1.201, which gives a figure of 0.895. This represents a fall of 10.5% (1−0.895 = 0.105).

Since percentage change in the Cg reflects change in relative economic standing measured by growth in a country's GDP per capita relative to the growth in world GDP per capita, all countries growing at a rate slower than the world average are lagging behind and their relative economic position is worsening, and, conversely, countries with faster GDP per capita growth than the world average are improving their relative economic position and this is reflected by an increase in the value of the Cg.

The data for 1990, 2000, 2005, 2009, and 2014 used in this study are World Bank data on GDP at current prices in 2005 constant US$ and population figures from the World Bank database. They are available on the World Bank website.[3]

3.2 Economic Growth and Changes in the Relative Balance of Economic Power: 1990–2000

The final decade of the twentieth century saw a number of very important historical changes in global political relations. These directly produced further changes in many countries' economic systems, resulting in their integration into international trade in goods and services and international capital flows. These changes were strongly related to the disappearance of the former so-called socialist bloc ("the Eastern Bloc"), led by the former

USSR, and so the formation of the Newly Independent States and the restoration of autonomy in the countries of Central and Eastern Europe and their transition towards democratic political arrangements and market economy. It was during this period that the longest war on European soil since the Second World War took place, namely the war against Bosnia and Herzegovina (1992–1995), as a consequence of the dissolution of the former Yugoslavia.

The period from 1990 to 2000 also saw the Maastricht treaty and the Stability and Growth Pact between the countries of the European Community, providing the basis for its transformation into the EU. The founding of the European Central Bank (1998) was followed by the introduction of the first regional common currency – the euro (1999). This has without doubt had (and will continue to have) far-reaching consequences. From a theoretical perspective, it was the first practical application and testing of the theory of optimal currency areas, introduced into the literature by Robert Mundell.[4] The introduction of a common currency for the initial 11 member countries of the Eurozone was preceded by unconditional implementation of full-scale financial liberalization for all member countries, the legislative basis for which was provided by the European Single Act and the Maastricht treaty. The 1990s also saw three major financial crises: the so-called Tequila crisis in Mexico (1994), the South-East Asian crisis of 1997–1998, and the Russian rouble crisis (1998). The South-East Asian crisis was of greater proportions and had considerably greater consequences.

The 1990s, and in particular their second half, were a period of greater economic prosperity for the US economy than the preceding three decades had been. Rates of economic (and productivity) growth were high, particularly in the technology sector (the IT industry), and provided a basis for major inflows of capital as portfolio investment in US companies, again primarily in IT, particularly given the steep outflow of capital caused by the South-East Asian and the Russian rouble crises. Growing confidence in the strength of the US economy and its corporate sector saw share prices in that sector rising sharply. By the end of the decade, or more precisely the end of October 2000 (by when the common European currency had been in existence for more than 20 months), the dollar peaked against the euro, with one dollar worth a little more than EUR1.21. The rise in share prices in the United States came to an abrupt end with the implosion of the dot-com bubble in the second half of 2000. While the US economy was dominating the 1990s,

Table 3.2 Ten fastest-growing economies in the world: 1990–2000

Country	*Percentage change in Cg 2000/1990*
China	110.9
Cabo Verde	104.6
Ireland	59.4
Vietnam	53.5
Republic of Korea	49.3
Isle of Man	43.2
Lebanon	38.7
Chile	38.2
Guyana	36.5
Malta	35.4

Source: Calculated by the author using World Bank data.

the Japanese economy was marked by stagnation and preoccupied with "cleaning-up" the balance sheets of the major Japanese banks, which had dominated the world of global banking through the 1980s.

Based on our analysis of changes in relative economic power across the world, measured by the Cg, the group of ten fastest-growing economies included the following countries.

Note: Equatorial Guinea and Swaziland were, in fact, the two fastest-growing economies, with increases in the Cg of 872% and 634%, respectively, but have been excluded from the table as absolute outliers.

From Table 3.2 we see that the group of fastest-growing economies during the final ten years of the twentieth century did not include a single country in transition. This is hardly surprising, as the 1990s were the first years of transition, a period that entailed radical change to their political, institutional, economic, and social orders and therefore a decade of adjusting to entirely new rules of the game. Most of these countries, and particularly those that had been part of the Soviet Union or the SFRY, saw major falls in GDP per capita and impoverishment during this decade. The countries with the greatest relative decline (the percentage drop in the Cg is in brackets) were: Tajikistan (–71.6), Moldova (–68.6), Georgia (–64.6), DR Congo (–63.7), Ukraine (–60.2), Azerbaijan (–54.5), Kyrgyz Republic (–48.1), Turkmenistan (–44.3), Russian Federation (–40.8), and Djibouti (–40.8).

In 1990, the five countries with the highest GDP per capita had an average Cg of 11.65. The average for the five poorest was 0.03. They were: Monaco, Liechtenstein, Bermuda, Luxembourg and Switzerland,

and Uganda, Malawi, Mozambique, Liberia, and Ethiopia, respectively. These values for the Cg indicate that GDP per capita in the five richest countries was 11.65 times the world average (or 1165%), while it was approximately one 33rd (or just 3%) of the world average in the five poorest.

During the last decade of the twentieth century, differences in the distribution of newly produced goods and services (GDP) increased. Thanks to gradual and controlled opening-up to long-term capital flows based on inward (export-oriented) FDI, some of the poorest countries did succeed in boosting growth rates and reducing the gap from the world average. This reduction in their poverty could not compensate, however, for the major reduction in new wealth creation in a larger group of countries (namely the countries in transition and undeveloped countries). This led to rising economic inequality worldwide, certainly in comparison to the beginning of the decade. The list of the top five countries ranked by GDP per capita had barely changed by 2000. The five countries with the highest Cg that year were: Monaco, Lichtenstein, Luxembourg, Bermuda, and Norway. The five poorest countries were: Ethiopia, Burundi, Liberia, the Democratic Republic of Congo, and Rwanda.

In the last year of the twentieth century, the difference between the average Cg for the five wealthiest and that for the five poorest countries had increased compared to 1990 by 37.8%. Consequently in spite of the high rates of real economic growth in the group of fastest-growing countries, which at this point did include a number of developing countries (particularly China and Vietnam), the way in which the majority of other developing countries increasingly fell behind over the final decade of the last century, in combination with the continued impoverishment of poor and highly indebted countries and the sharp economic decline of the countries in transition which had previously been part of the former Soviet Union, produced a marked growth in inequality worldwide.

3.3 Economic Growth and Changes to the Relative Economic Power: 2000–2014

The period 2000–2014 can be divided into two phases, at least for the world of international relations and the global flows of goods, services, and capital. The first phase was the period 2000–2008, which saw sharp economic expansion on the part of the oil-producing nations, high growth rates for the countries in transition as a consequence of financial and trade liberalization, and particularly steep growth in lending by internationally active banks (the global megabanks), accompanied by an even more spectacular increase in turnover on the financial derivatives market. According to data from the Bank for International Settlements, between 2002 and 2008 lending by internationally active banks grew at twice the rate it had between 1985 and 2002.[5]

The second phase followed the major financial shock that began in the United States in August 2007 but worsened progressively through 2008, before spilling over to Europe and other parts of the world in the final quarter of that year and the first quarter of 2009. This period from 2008 to 2014 was marked primarily by major changes in how the most-developed countries, and in particular the United States, United Kingdom, Japan, and the countries of the Eurozone, conduct their economic policy (monetary and fiscal policy in the first place). A highly expansionary monetary and fiscal policy marked a return to the Keynes's recipe book for conducting economic policy during periods of significant downturn in the business cycle, with sharp falls in the volume of international trade in goods and services and major falls in the prices of financial assets on the leading world stock exchanges. Nor were the developing countries spared the impact of these financial and economic shocks, which spilled over first from the United States to Western Europe and Japan, and then from the countries of Western Europe and Japan to other parts of the world.

In contrast to the final decade of the twentieth century, during this period, it was now the transition and developing countries that made up the largest sub-category within the group of 20 fastest-growing economies. In comparing the economic results achieved during these two periods, we must always keep in mind that the transition countries had come into being as a category because of the collapse of the former USSR, due to which they had experienced major falls in GDP per capita. This was why they accounted for eight of the ten countries with the greatest falls in their Cg during that period. Of those eight, four were later members of the group of the fastest-growing economies in the world in the subsequent period: Azerbaijan (the fastest-growing economy), Tajikistan, Georgia, and Turkmenistan.

As the fastest-growing economy in the world during the first fourteen years of this century, Azerbaijan managed to increase GDP per capita by a factor of 3.75. Its main export was oil, the rising price of which played a

Table 3.3 Twenty fastest-growing economies in the world: 2000–2014

Country	*Percentage change in Cg - 2014/2000*
Azerbaijan	212.0
China	185.4
Macao, SAR China	178.3
Turkmenistan	129.7
Armenia	121.4
Equatorial Guinea	117.7
Mongolia	105.8
Kazakhstan	98.1
Belarus	97.9
Ethiopia	91.3
Cambodia	88.2
Angola	85.5
Georgia	84.2
India	81.8
Uzbekistan	79.2
Chad	78.6
Tajikistan	77.8
Lao PDR	76.2
Bhutan	73.3
Latvia	72.3

Source: Calculated by the author using World Bank data.

leading role in the growth of the Azerbaijani economy. During the same period, China saw GDP per capita rise by a factor of 3.43. Even with such growth, Chinese GDP per capita was still approximately half of world average GDP in 2014 (as indicated by China's Cg of 0.484 for that year). As Table 3.3 makes clear, if one excludes Macao, as a small and highly specific economy whose core revenues come from tourism and games of fortune, 18 of the remaining 19 fastest-growing economies during these fourteen years come from the group of developing or low-income countries (Latvia being the exception). In 2014, the average Cg of these 19 (again excluding Macao) was 0.395. At the beginning of the century, it had been 0.194. In other words, they had narrowed the gap between the world average GDP and their average GDP per capita from around 5.2:1 to 2.5:1.

In the final decade of the last century the group of 20 fastest-growing economies had included as many as ten developed or middle-income developing countries. During the first fourteen years of this century, it included only two: namely Macao, a high-income country, and Latvia, a country in transition that only graduated to the group of advanced countries in 2014. Even though Equatorial Guinea enjoyed a higher Cg than Latvia in 2014, it was not included amongst the group of advanced countries, because its HDI (Human Development Index) was 39.5% lower than Latvia's.

The United Arab Emirates was one of the ten countries to see the greatest fall in their Cg in 2014 against 2000. In fact, it was the greatest fall in the Cg of all, down by 53.3%. While it still belongs to the group of advanced countries, this fall in the Cg was primarily due to population growth, which has been faster than anywhere else in the world: its population more than tripled in just fourteen years (from 3.1 to 9.4 million).[6] As a consequence of the greatest economic crisis in the developed world in seventy years and of poor economic policy (and policy more generally), Italy also found itself one of the ten countries with the greatest falls in their Cg (and so GDP per capita). Italy's GDP per capita (which is a member of the G-7) was down 8.05% (measured in 2005 constant US$), while its Cg declined by 23.4%. Other countries that experienced major falls in their Cg included Greece and Cyprus, with drops of 18.5% and 17.1%, respectively.

The global financial crisis of 2008 and the Great Recession resulted in falling Cg in most of the advanced countries. The group of 20 worst performers in the world included developed or high-income countries like Italy, Portugal, Cyprus, Greece, and the United Arab Emirates. One important reason for this was the recession in Western Europe, the United States, and the other advanced economies. Certain countries of the EU had seen recession not just in 2009, but also in 2012 and 2013 (mainly in the southern part of Eurozone). Every single country from the EU-15 group recorded negative rates of change in the Cg: Sweden (–0.5), Germany (–2.1), United Kingdom (–3.8), Austria (–5.2), Ireland (–5.8), Finland (–7.0), Belgium (–9.0), the Netherlands (–9.8), France (–10.9), Luxembourg (–11.3), Spain (–12.3), Denmark (–14.6), Portugal (–17.0), Greece (–18.5), and Italy (–23.4).[7] The average rate at which the Cg fell for the EU-15 countries was 10.1%, with a standard deviation of 6.44. The countries that suffered the largest relative falls were Italy (by almost a quarter of its standing in 2000), Greece, and Portugal. These countries also saw falls in GDP per capita (and therefore not only a relative but also an absolute fall in growth). By contrast, a group of countries starting with Sweden and ending with Denmark actually experienced a rise in GDP per capita. This was a smaller rise in percentage terms than the increase in world GDP per capita, so that even these countries were falling behind the average level of growth in the world economy.

The EU-13 saw an average rate of Cg growth between 2000 and 2014 of 25.9%, with a standard deviation of 27.8. This clearly indicates the major differences in actual rates of Cg growth in these countries, which is to say the very uneven change in relative economic standing. Ignoring for the moment Malta and Cyprus, the only two countries of the EU-13 group to have experienced significant deterioration of their relative economic standing during the period in question, the average rate of Cg growth in the other ten non-core EU countries was 33.5%, with a standard deviation of 23.3. Given the range in population size in the various EU-13 countries, it is worth pointing out that the most populous economy in the group, Poland, actually recorded very significant progress. The fastest-growing countries in this group, expressed in percentage increase in the Cg, were: Latvia (72.3), Romania (55.1), Bulgaria (47.2), Estonia (44.7), Slovak Republic (43.9), Poland (36.9), followed by Czech Republic (13.7), Hungary (11.0), Croatia (6.8), and Slovenia (3.9).

3.4 Relative Economic Performance In The World: A Brief Look By Continent

A look at the changes in relative economic standing by continent reveals that during the analytical period the poorest continent was consistently Africa, with average Cg for 1990, 2000, and 2014 of 0.208, 0.226, and 0.259, respectively. The values of these coefficients for the relevant years reveal that, while the continental average value for GDP per capita was one fifth the world average in 1990, the gap was reduced over the following quarter century to 2014, as the coefficient rose from a fifth to a quarter. On the other hand, Africa is the only continent to have seen the gap between the richest 25% and the poorest 25% of countries on the continent itself increase (Table 3.4).

The continent with the smallest gap between the richest 25% and the poorest 25% of countries is South America, but one should remember that there are relatively few countries on the continent compared to either Asia or Europe (about a quarter). Even here, the gap between the richest 25% and the poorest 25% of countries went up, both in the last decade of the last century and the first fourteen years of this one. The most successful continent in reducing the gap between the richest 25% and the poorest 25%

Table 3.4 Average relative economic growth by continent: 1990–2000–2014

Continents	*Year*		
	1990	*2000*	*2014*
Africa			
Average Cg	0.208	0.226	0.259
Top Quartile/Low Quartile Aver. Cg	14.9	19.6	20.2
Asia			
Average Cg	1.050	1.237	1.334
Top Quartile/Low Quartile Aver. Cg	45.2	57.5	40.7
Australia and Oceania			
Average Cg	0.982	0.969	0.949
Top Quartile/Low Quartile Aver. Cg	13.4	17.1	18.6
Europe			
Average Cg	3.940	2.876	2.792
Top Quartile/Low Quartile Aver. Cg	24.0	27.3	14.7
North America			
Average Cg	1.847	1.771	1.634
Top Quartile/Low Quartile Aver. Cg	17.1	19.1	16.2
South America			
Average Cg	0.502	0.518	0.622
Top Quartile/Low Quartile Aver. Cg	4.5	4.9	5.5

Source: Calculated by the author using World Bank data

between 2000 and 2014 was Europe, where the difference in average Cg for the top 25% and the bottom 25% was cut by almost a half (from 27.3:1 to 14.7:1). During the final decade of the last century, Asia was the continent with the most rapidly growing gap between the richest and the poorest 25%. During the first fourteen years of this century, the gap narrowed by approximately a quarter, so that the difference was actually lower in 2014 than it had been in 1990.

3.5 Inequalities in the Distribution of World Income: 1990–2014

In the second part of his book, *The Great Escape*,[8] the winner of the 2015 Nobel Prize for economics, Angus Deaton, offers an analysis of US economic performance and of inequalities in the distribution of income there, as well as the impact globalization has had on economic growth and the distribution of world income. His preferred methodological approach to measuring the distribution of income across the various countries in the world is to take income measured in US dollars' purchasing power parity (US$ PPP) for each country, but he also makes clear a series of problems and objections analysts face in trying to express national income in purchasing power parity terms. Given the problems involved in gathering all the relevant data on prices and household consumption in every country in the world needed to calculate purchasing power parity coefficients for each country separately, the result is a good deal of imprecision and general mess. Nonetheless, in spite of these shortcomings, Deaton insists that presenting differences in national income in terms of US$ PPP is still the methodologically best way to go about measuring inequality at the global level.

Taking Deaton's clear statement as to the need to analyze differences in actual incomes across the world as my starting point, I have in this part of the text calculated a series of values for national income coefficients (Cni), based on each country's share in world GNI expressed in US$ PPP in current prices for 1990, 2000 and 2014 for the countries for which data on GNI in US$ PPP are available in the World Bank database.[9] For our purposes of measuring inequalities in the distribution of income around the world, I have calculated the Cni as the ratio of a country's share in world GNI expressed in US$ PPP to its share in world population. Naturally, GNI for the three years in question is greater when measured in US$ PPP in current prices than it would have been measured in the current prices and nominal exchange rates. The calculations reveal that the differential between the average Cni arranged by quartile and by decile was greater in 2014 than in 2000 and greater in 2000 than in 1990. This growing gap is, moreover, largely due to increased concentration of wealth in countries of the highest decile (decile 10), particularly in comparison to the countries in the lowest decile (decile 1).

Data on the values for average Cni by quartile and by decile for the 150 countries for which data was available in 1990 reveal a difference in the average Cni of the 10 richest and the 10 poorest countries of almost 55:1, while that between the 10th decile and the 1st decile was approximately 43:1, and that between the 4th (top) and the 1st (lowest) quartile was approximately 23:1. The largest Cni differentials *within* the different quartiles or deciles were those in the first and fourth quartiles and in the first decile. These differentials are presented in the following Table 3.5,

Table 3.5 Average national income coefficient (Cni) based on GNI in US$ PPP by quartile and decile: World in 1990

	Average Cni 1990	*Standard deviation*
World Average	1.410	1.579
Quartile 4 Average	3.727	1.405
Quartile 3 Average	1.190	0.311
Quartile 2 Average	0.494	0.159
Quartile 1 Average	0.162	0.052
Top Quartile/Lowest Quartile	23.0	
Decile 10	4.867	1.514
Decile 9	3.372	0.365
Decile 8	2.003	0.322
Decile 7	1.243	0.135
Decile 6	0.915	0.061
Decile 5	0.683	0.087
Decile 4	0.440	0.058
Decile 3	0.280	0.042
Decile 2	0.181	0.017
Decile 1	0.114	0.031

Source: Calculated by the author using World Bank data.

which gives both the average values of the Cni and the values of the standard deviations for each group of countries.

The ten richest countries in the world on the basis of GNI per capita expressed in US$ PPP (in current prices) in 1990 were: Brunei Darussalam, Luxembourg, Switzerland, Bermuda, Macao, Saudi Arabia, the United States, Oman, Singapore, and Iceland. Their average GNI per capita in US$ PPP was 5.37 times the world average. The ten poorest countries were: Mozambique, Malawi, Ethiopia, Uganda, Burkina Faso, Rwanda, Swaziland, Niger, Central African Republic, and Burundi. Their average Cni was 0.098, so their average GNI per capita in US$ PPP was approximately one tenth of the world average. China and India were both among the 20 poorest countries in the world, with GNI per capita of approximately one fifth of the world average.

By 2000, these differences in the distribution of income worldwide had grown, as measured by the ratio of the average Cni for the richest 10% (decile 10) and the poorest 10% (decile 1) of countries. This gap was up from 43:1 in 1990 to approximately 52:1. The ten countries with the highest GNI per capita were: Kuwait, Brunei Darussalam, Luxembourg, Singapore, the United States, Switzerland, Norway, Bahrain, Oman, and

Table 3.6 Average national income coefficient (Cni) based on GNI in US$ PPP by quartile and decile: World in 2000

	Average Cni 2000	*Standard deviation*	*Standard deviation in percentage of Cni*
Quartile 4	3.553	1.516	42.67
Quartile 3	1.012	0.263	25.95
Quartile 2	0.380	0.118	30.98
Quartile 1	0.133	0.050	37.78
Decile10	4.830	1.482	30.68
Decile 9	3.020	0.498	16.47
Decile 8	1.626	0.278	17.08
Decile 7	1.111	0.111	9.98
Decile 6	0.825	0.065	7.92
Decile 5	0.615	0.090	14.58
Decile 4	0.404	0.051	12.56
Decile 3	0.268	0.031	11.69
Decile 2	0.175	0.032	18.09
Decile 1	0.088	0.024	27.22

Source: Calculated by the author using World Bank data.

Macao. The gap between the 25% richest and the 25% poorest countries in the world had not changed much against 1990, however. China had pushed up its GNI per capita from 19.8% to 37.7% of the world average, while India achieved 26.6% of the world average (Table 3.6).

The greatest difference in income within a quartile was between the richest 25% of countries in the world, in which the standard deviation from the average Cni for that quartile was approximately 42.7%. The smallest difference was in the third quartile. The greatest difference by decile was in the richest 10%, the smallest in the sixth decile. In 2000, the poorest 10% of countries lagged even further behind average global GNI – whereas in 1990 average world GNI per capita had been approximately 10 times their average, now it was 11.4 times. In other words, in this group of countries, average GNI per capita was just 8.8% of average world GNI per capita in US$ PPP in 2000.

The 2000–2014 was the period of most intensive financial globalization in modern history. By 2014, the ratio in income distribution between the richest and the poorest 10% of countries had risen against 2000 from 52:1 to 54:1. The difference between the ten richest and the ten poorest countries also grew significantly, from 76:1 to 83.5:1, while the average

GNI per capita of the poorest 10% had fallen from 8.8% to 8.3% of world GNI per capita. The biggest differences within quartiles were to be found in the group of the 25% richest and the 25% poorest countries. The greatest differences within deciles were also in the groups of the richest 10% and the poorest 10%.

Azerbaijan realized the greatest relative growth in GNI per capita in the period from 2000 to 2014. As the fastest-growing economy in the period, it increased its Cni by 162% (its Cg increased by 212%). The second fastest-growing economy was China, whose Cni increased by 136.8%. During the period from 1990 to 2014, China managed to reduce its shortfall vis-à-vis world GNI per capita, climbing from 19.5% of the world average in 1990 to a level of 89.5% in 2014. Among the BRIC countries, Russia was the second fastest-growing economy during the fourteen years to 2014, its Cni up 75.5% on 2000, but nonetheless still 3.4% down on 1990. In the same period India improved its relative economic standing, measured in Cni, by 49.2%. It was, however, growing considerably more slowly than China, only reaching 39.1% of world GNI per capita by 2014, in contrast to China's 89.5%. In comparing the economic results of the two most populous countries in the world, however, one must keep in mind that India has seen considerably faster population growth. In the period of interest to us, India's total population has increased by 44%, compared to 19.6% in China (Table 3.7).

The average Cni of the most powerful economy in the world – the United States – fell by 21.6% in 2000–2014, in contrast to the growth its economy had enjoyed in the 1990–2000, when it had achieved its best results in three decades and its Cni had improved 3%. The United Kingdom and Japan also experienced very significant relative economic decline in the first fourteen years of this century, 25.9% and 24.5%, respectively. Within the EU, the countries that experienced the greatest relative decline in national income in those years were Italy (−31.4%), Greece (−26.9%), Spain (−20.2%) and Portugal (−16%). It is worth noting that the UK's relative decline in national income was more marked than Spain's or Portugal's.

Such changes in relative economic standing have resulted in Italy falling from 21st, which it held in 1990, to 31st place in the world, in terms of GNI per capita in US$ PPP. The United Kingdom fell from 19th to 26th, the United States from 5th to 11th, while Ireland improved its standing from 26th to 21st. As a country whose rapid economic growth in the final decade of the last century and the first five years of this one was based on intensive inflows of capital and one which has again been realizing very high capital

Table 3.7 Average national income coefficient (Cni) based on GNI in US$ PPP by quartiles and deciles: World in 2014

	Average Cni 2014	*Standard deviation*	*Standard deviation in percentage of Cni*
Quartile 4	3.133	1.535	48.99
Quartile 3	1.150	0.249	21.63
Quartile 2	0.498	0.156	31.18
Quartile 1	0.145	0.065	44.37
Decile10	4.482	1.659	37.01
Decile 9	2.536	0.317	12.49
Decile 8	1.666	0.156	9.39
Decile 7	1.244	0.106	8.55
Decile 6	0.924	0.096	10.42
Decile 5	0.666	0.085	12.75
Decile 4	0.428	0.064	14.99
Decile 3	0.277	0.046	16.75
Decile 2	0.162	0.033	20.31
Decile 1	0.083	0.025	30.50

Source: Calculated by the author using World Bank data.

inflows since 2010, the example of Ireland makes clear the major difference between such a country's ranking in terms of GDP per capita (as measured by the Cg) and its ranking in terms of GNI per capita (as measured by the Cni). Based on GDP per capita expressed in 2005 US$, Ireland was one of the ten highest GDP per capita countries in the world in 2014 – in fact it had the eighth largest GDP per capita measured in constant 2005 US$. Its GNI per capita based on US$ PPP, however, relegates it to 21st place. In other words, the disparity between actual total production of goods and services in the country and the revenues arising from that production because of the significant role of FDI and foreign capital in the Irish economy is indicative of the proportion of revenues represented by non-resident income.

At the end of this chapter on the specific position of the developed countries and changes in their relative and absolute economic standing, we can hardly avoid giving special mention to Germany. This country has succeeded in improving its world ranking measured by actual GNI per capita from 23rd in 2000 to 14th place in 2014. Even if its GNI per capita had declined from 3.5 times the world average in 2000 to 3.22 times it in 2014, so that relatively speaking there has been a reduction in growth, Germany is nonetheless the only country from the G-10 group of countries to have seen significant improvement in its relative ranking. By contrast, the second most important economy in the Eurozone, France fell from 22nd to 24th place.

Notes

1. The dollar figures in this section are all expressed in 2005 US$. For the author's calculations, see the Appendix.
2. Fikret Čaušević 2006/2008.
3. For GDP, see The World Bank: http://data.worldbank.org/indicator/NY.GDP.MKTP.KD?page=2, for population data, see The World Bank: http://data.worldbank.org/indicator/SP.POP.TOTL?page=2
4. Mundell 1961.
5. Bank for International Settlements 2010, pp. 6–7.
6. See the World Bank population data in the World Economic Indicators (WEI) for the relevant years or on the World Bank website: http://data.worldbank.org/indicator/SP.POP.TOTL
7. Calculated by the author using the World Bank database.
8. Deaton 2013.
9. See: http://data.worldbank.org/indicator/NY.GNP.MKTP.PP.CD?page=2

References

Bank for International Settlements. (2010). *Long-term issues in international banking* (CGFS Papers No. 41). Basel (July).

Čaušević, F. (2006). *Economic sovereignty and global capital flows.* Sarajevo: International Forum Bosnia.

Čaušević, F. (2008). *Economic sovereignty and global capital flows.* Hyderabad: Icfai, Hyderabad University Press.

Deaton, A. (2013). *The great escape – health, wealth, and the origins of inequality.* Princeton: Princeton University Press.

Mundell, R. (1961). A theory of optimum currency areas. *American Economic Review*, *51*(4), 657–665.

Websites:

The World Bank: http://data.worldbank.org/indicator/NY.GDP.MKTP.KD?page=2

The World Bank: http://data.worldbank.org/indicator/SP.POP.TOTL?page=2

The World Bank: http://data.worldbank.org/indicator/SP.POP.TOTL

CHAPTER 4

The Fastest-Growing Economies and Financial Openness

The analysis in Chapter 3 has shown that the group of the fastest-growing economies in the first fourteen years of this century comprised predominantly developing, transition or African countries. None of the 20 highest-ranking countries by the value of Cg were in the group. Indeed, almost all of them saw their relative economic standing (Cg) decline and some even experienced an absolute fall in GDP per capita.

Naturally enough, China and India, respectively the 3rd and 8th fastest-growing economies in the period 1990–2014, were both in the group, recording improvements in their Cg of 501.8% and 126.7%, respectively. Otherwise, the group comprised essentially two subcategories:

(1) Countries in transition, which experienced major relative decline in the decade up to 2000, but joined the fastest-growing economies in the fourteen years after
(2) Extremely poor countries, which succeeded in improving both their relative and absolute economic indicators, but, given their extremely low baseline level of GDP per capita in 2000, still had not crossed the "poverty threshold" by 2014.

These economic developments since 2000 reveal a major paradox in the relationship between financial openness and economic growth. Nearly 75% of global capital flows were between rich countries. This includes not just FDI and portfolio investment, but also bank loans and transactions in

F. Čaušević, *A Study into Financial Globalization, Economic Growth and (In)Equality*, DOI 10.1007/978-3-319-51403-1_4

financial derivatives. The significant relative decline of the rich countries, as measured by the Cg, indicates a negative correlation between the amount and value of these financial flows between developed countries and the efficiency with which they are being used. This paradox of financial globalization was particularly evident during the 2000s and its underlying sources connected with the major weakening of the system of external and internal controls over the use of flows based on lending and derivatives transactions, often themselves directly derived from commercial bank credit activities (e.g. expansion of the credit default swap market).

Capital flows from 2000 to 2014 (and in some cases already from 1980 to 2000) meant that the United States, the United Kingdom, China, and a number of small open economies like Ireland and Hong Kong were amongst the leading net-recipient countries of FDI and portfolio equity flows.

4.1 China – Economic Growth and Financial Openness

Unique among the 20 fastest-growing economies from 2000 to 2014, China was one of the five fastest-growing economies in every five-year period from 1990 to 2014, improving its relative economic standing (Cg) by an impressive 501.8%. This made it the third fastest-growing economy in the world during that period, after Equatorial Guinea and Swaziland, whose rates of relative economic (Cg) growth were 2017% and 604.3%, respectively. Its Cg improved 110.9% in the ten years to 2000, 42.3% for 2000–2005, 47.3% for the following four years, and 36.1% from 2009 to 2014 (see data in the Appendix).

The Chinn-Ito index measures de jure financial openness.[1] The value of Ka_open for China did not change between 1993 and 2014 (when the updated database ends), standing at 0.1638 (normalized value 16.38) for the entire period.[2] This classifies China as relatively de jure financially closed, reflecting significant limitations imposed by the Chinese government on the free movement of short-term capital and partial restrictions on current account openness. Strict supervision and regulation of the exchange rate policy has played an important role in China's macroeconomic policy. The policy between 1995 and 2005 was based upon a fixed exchange rate (US$1 = CNY8.3). Since transitioning to a managed float (in 2005), the Chinese authorities have allowed a gradual appreciation in the yuan, but controlled and directed towards maintaining Chinese producer price competitiveness abroad and the target rate of economic growth at home, based on a policy of export and investment-led growth. Appreciation between early 2006 and 2009 was a little more than 18%.[3] Since recession struck the developed countries (2009), the Chinese authorities have kept a de facto fixed exchange rate of 6.83 yuan to the US$. In March 2015, it hit a twenty-year peak (US$1/CNY6.20), but the Chinese authorities engineered a depreciation of 5.5% during the second half of 2015.

Although formally a relatively closed economy on the basis of the Chinn-Ito index, it would be very wrong to conclude that China owes its exceptional economic results over the past twenty-five years to financial repression as such. What the low Chinn-Ito index really reflects is a carefully calibrated and directed financial opening-up to long-term capital flows, particularly to FDI flows. Thanks to financial incentives for foreign direct investors, the low cost of labour, and a high degree of working discipline, China had succeeded in attracting foreign investors into export-oriented projects and so in becoming the largest exporter of goods in the world by 2010. One consequence of this financial opening-up has been the growth in assets reported in China's International Investment Position, from US$1,223.3 billion in 2005 to US$6,408.7 billion in 2014, while its total liabilities rose from US$815.6 billion to US$4,623.3 billion (source given below Fig. 4.1).

The time series data for total assets and liabilities presented in the International Investment Position Statement (2004–2014) shows that China was a net exporter of capital throughout that period. In other words, its net international investment position (NIIP) was positive. Assets exceeded liabilities by US$407.7 billion in 2004[4] and by as much as US$1,776.4 billion by the end of 2014. Foreign exchange reserves were the main item in the composition of China's total assets, up from US$611 billion in 2004 to US$3,993 billion in June 2014.[5] By contrast, during the ten years to 2000, they had risen from US$30 billion to just US$166 billion. Moreover, in spite of rapid growth of the external debt, from US$145.6 billion in 2000 to US$959.5 billion in 2014, the external debt to GDP ratio actually fell, from 12.1% to 9.3%.[6] The degree of de facto financial openness, as measured by TOTAL (a country's total assets plus liabilities presented through the country's international investment position over GDP), reveals both a major inflow of foreign capital into the country and major holdings (assets) by the country abroad. China's

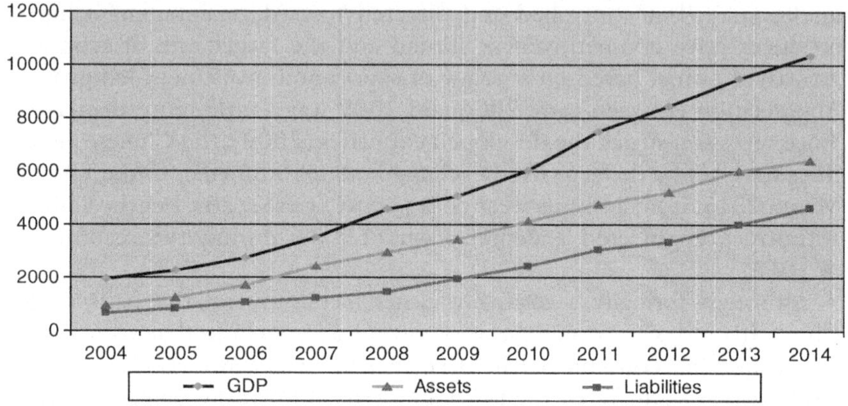

Fig. 4.1 China's international investment position: 2004–2014 (in billions of US$)

Source: http://www.safe.gov.cn/wps/wcm/connect/11518a004f5a09699f869f219f90791c/IIP.xls?MOD=AJPERES&CACHEID=11518a004f5a09699f869f219f90791c (accessed on 12 May 2016)

TOTAL measure of financial openness scores were 89.9%, 106.4%, and 106.6% for 2005, 2009 and 2014, respectively.[7]

In 2014, China' TOTAL score was 4.6 times lower than Germany's and 3.1 times lower than the United States'. Total capital investment and particularly net FDI inflows, however, reveal that China was nonetheless one of the most important destinations for foreign investors during the fourteen years preceding. Total net FDI inflows into China between 1981 and 1990 had been a very modest US$18.3 billion. Between 1990 and 2000, they rose to US$318 billion and the amount invested in China in the 2001–2014 was US$2,246 billion. Net FDI to China was particularly strong between 2010 and 2014, at US$1,345 billion.[8] In contrast to this openness to FDI (as the basis for export-led growth), capital flows on the basis of net portfolio equity investment were considerably less, reflecting restrictions on short-term and to some degree on long-term capital flows (captured by the Chinn-Ito de jure measure of financial openness), which were related to an attempt to protect Chinese capital markets from potential speculative capital "attacks". Major financial shocks have, nonetheless, been generated "internally", through the formation of financial bubbles in 2006–2007 and, more especially, in 2014–2015, as Chinese residents'

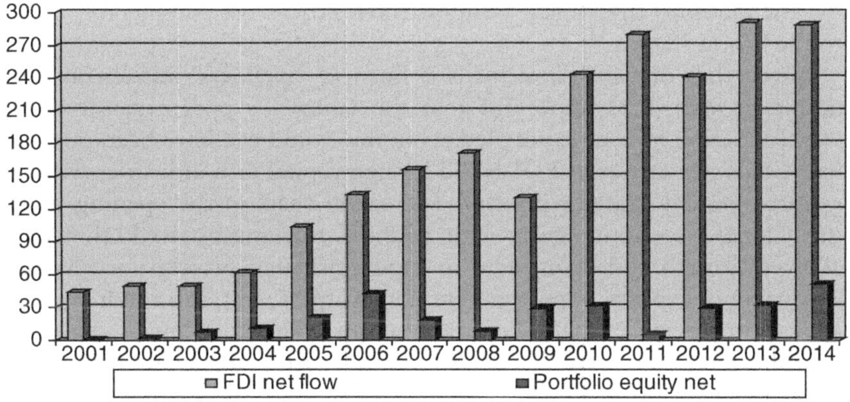

Fig. 4.2 FDI and portfolio equity net capital flows to China: 2001–2014 (in billions of US$)

Source: The World Bank http://data.worldbank.org/indicator; http://data.worldbank.org/indicator/BX.KLT.DINV.CD.WD?page=1

growing appetites for risk and expectations of quick profits from capital gains led to the formation of the largest financial bubble since the US dot-com bubble in 1999/2000 (Fig. 4.2).

While growth in net FDI to China in the eight years to 2008 was very strongly positively correlated with GDP growth, this correlation weakened considerably between 2009 and 2014. The correlation coefficient between the two variables for 2001–2005 was 0.92, for 2006–2010 it was 0.71, and for 2011–2014 it declined to 0.44 (non-overlapping periods).[9] Although the correlation coefficient is a simple statistical indicator and has well-known limitations for the analysis of economic variables, these values are nonetheless indicative of very significant and growing problems facing the Chinese economy which will no doubt continue in coming years.

This analysis of net FDI and GDP in China is based exclusively on World Bank data. There are significant differences between the World Bank database and the United Nations Conference on Trade and Development (UNCTAD) one regarding net FDI inflows to China. The UNCTAD data show significantly lower net FDI inflows to China, but even on the basis of them China remains a leading destination for 2013–2014, outstripping net FDI flows to the United States. In any case, Chinese government data from the International Investment Position 2004–2015[10] are considerably closer to the World Bank's.[11]

Given that our analytical focus is financial openness' impact on economic growth, it is important that the China's export expansion and transformation into an export-led economy would not have been possible had China not attracted FDI-based foreign capital into industries with an export-oriented strategic priority. The causal chain in the opening-up of the Chinese economy starts with financial opening-up to FDI, which allowed growth and investment in export-oriented projects, accelerated expansion of exports, a merchandise trade surplus, and, as a result, a sharp growth in foreign exchange reserves, which China then invested abroad (the allocated FX reserves have been primarily used for the purchase of US government securities).

The strategy to attract FDI and so promote export-led growth was (and still is) set out in five-year development plans (China's Five Year Plan), the law on FDI, and the catalogue for the guidance of foreign investments in industries.[12] According to the US State Department, the catalogue was last updated in May 2015. The catalogue clearly sets out the Chinese government understanding of its strategy for attracting FDI into target industries with the primary goal of increasing exports.

China is the only country since the Second World War to have succeeded in maintaining very high rates of economic growth over so long a period as twenty-five years. Since 2010, however, real rates of growth have been declining. One important root of this problem is the efficiency of both forms of investment: foreign direct and domestic. The fall in the correlation coefficient of net FDI and GDP over the past five years corresponds to a growth in the proportion of GDP going to gross investment during that period, compared to either of the previous five-year periods (Fig. 4.3).

The share of China's GDP going to gross investment went up from 35.9% in 2001 to 40.5% in 2005 and 47.3% in 2011, falling back again to 45.8% in 2014. Gross investment thus accounted for a considerably higher proportion of GDP creation than household consumption over the entire period from 2005 to 2014. If China's investment-and-export-led growth model led to the sharp expansion in exports from 2000 to 2010 with a direct impact on expansion in foreign exchange reserves, it was also reflected in net exports' strongly growing role in GDP creation – up from 2.1% in 2001 to 8.7% in 2007 (its peak). Between 2008 and 2014, however, net exports fell to just 2.8% of GDP. Such trends might, at first glance, suggest China has gradually changed its model of economic

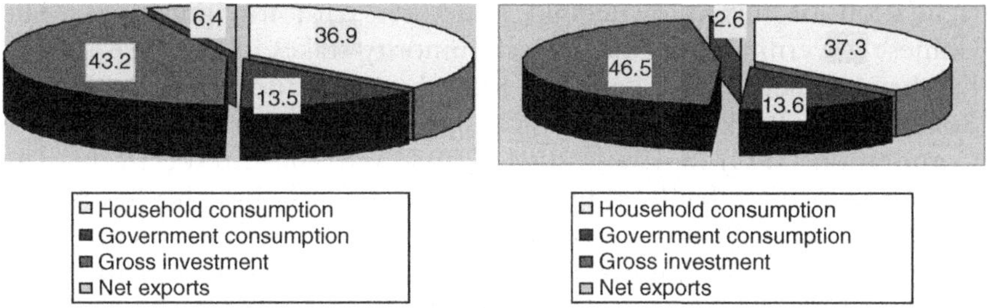

Fig. 4.3 Composition of China's GDP by expenditures for 2006–2010 and 2011–2014 (left and right pie, respectively) (shares in percentage points; yearly averages for the periods)

Source: The United Nations http://data.un.org/Data.aspx?d=SNAAMA&f=grID%3A101%3BcurrID%3AUSD%3BpcFlag%3A0 (accessed on 16 May 2016)

growth from an export-led to a domestic demand-led one, but data on household consumption's share in GDP do not support this idea. Rather, as already suggested, while investment has been kept at a very high proportion of GDP creation, its effectiveness has been falling. Such trends have already contributed to both a falling growth rate and a growing share of bad loans in banking sector total assets.

The Chinese economy's increasing integration into global financial and trade flows during the 1990–2014 (but particularly from 2000 to 2014) has been reflected in the sharp growth of the Chinese banking sector. In 2014–2015, Chinese banks have taken the top four spots on the list of the ten largest banks in the world, at least in terms of assets: the Industrial and Commercial Bank of China, the China Construction Bank, the Agricultural Bank of China, and the Bank of China. The sum of their assets in 2015 was US$12 trillion, some 3% more than Chinese GDP.[13] The total assets of the ten largest Chinese banks amounted to US$18.1 trillion in 2015, approximately equal to US GDP that year. From the global financial crisis to 2014, Chinese banks were facing an increase in non-performing loans, but analyzes of the DBS Group Research suggest the rate of increase in non-performing loans was down in 2015, thanks to simplified write-off procedures.[14] According to the same source, the level of non-performing loans at Chinese banks is expected to stabilize at around 2% in 2016–2017.

China's gradualist approach to financial liberalization and opening-up its banking sector to foreign capital is also discernible in its gradual facilitation of mixed ownership structures with foreign banks. The Chinese government decided to sell minority stakes in the CEB (China Everbright Bank), the Bank of Shanghai, the Industrial Bank, and BoCom (the Bank of Communications) to the International Finance Corporation (IFC) in 1999, 2001, 2003, and 2004, respectively. The IFC stake in these banks ranges from 2.5% to 15%, but this has been a very important step in the gradual "mixing" of ownership structures and improving the procedures and quality of corporate governance and decision-making. Between 2005 and 2008, the Chinese government also attracted a number of major private banking groups from the West to join the ownership structures of certain leading or fast-growing Chinese banks. HSBC Holding became owner of 8% of the Bank of Shanghai's equity in 2001 and of 19.9% of BoCom in 2004. In 2005, BNP Paribas bought a 19.2% stake in the Bank of Nanjing, while, in 2006, Goldman Sachs and Allianz bought 5.75% and 2.25%, respectively, of the stock of what is now the largest bank in the world – ICBC (the Industrial and Commercial Bank of China). In 2006, the Deutsche Bank bought 13.98% of the Hua Xia Bank, while, the same year, Citigroup bought 19.99% of the Guangfa Bank.[15]

The Chinese authorities continued to control interest rates and set "ceiling" rates on deposits and loans right up to 2013. They deregulated the rates on loans in 2013, but only did the same for deposits in October 2015.[16] These measures were a key step towards meeting IMF conditions for the yuan to become the fifth world reserve currency, joining the US$, the euro, the Japanese yen, and the British Pound. These are the currencies used to determine the value of the Special Drawing Rights and in which IMF country-member central banks can hold foreign currency reserves. The IMF Board of Governors made this historic decision to include the yuan at a session held on the last day of November in 2015.[17]

Parallel to this gradual financial liberalization and steep expansion of exports, based upon intensive courting of FDI and domestic investment financed by loans from the fast-growing Chinese banks, Chinese capital markets' importance for world market capitalization has also grown. The first great investment "boom" on the Chinese (Shanghai and Shenzhen) stock exchanges took place in 2006 and 2007, when China became the second largest capital market in the world by market capitalization. This financial bubble imploded in 2008, as the Chinese shares in the representative index lost more than half their market value. Between 2011 and 2014, the main Chinese index, the Shanghai-Shenzhen 300 Composite, was stagnating or even losing value, only to jump 145.6% between the beginning of June 2014 and mid-June 2015.[18] This was the largest financial bubble since the US dot-com bubble, fifteen years ago.

The extent of "irrational exuberance" (to borrow Greenspan's term from his lecture in December 1996) in China is clear from the erratic movements of the Shanghai-Shenzhen CSI 300, which was up almost 50% in just the first five months of 2015, while the American DJIA was keeping steady or falling slightly. The financial shock over the following two months (the second half of June to August 2015) helped cause a fall in the value of the stock contained in the DJIA. Such index movements in periods of crisis reveal a very high positive correlation at such times between the movements of the stock prices contained in the major world indices, in this case the DJIA and SSCI300. It was even more obvious during the final quarter of 2008 and the first quarter of 2009. Such movements show how mutually dependent the economies of the United States and China have become. The Chinese government and the People's Bank of China were the main actors in preventing an even greater fall in stock prices and market capitalization on Chinese capital markets. The People's Bank of China had deployed more than US$500 billion by the end of December 2015 in interventions on capital markets to prop up the value of the SSCI at a level around 3000. This scale of intervention resulted in a decline in Chinese foreign exchange reserves from a record level of nearly US$4 trillion in June 2014 to around US$3.3 trillion in early 2016.[19]

The Chinese economy's impressive economic growth over the last twenty-five years, measured in GDP per capita and our Cg, made China the second largest world economy in terms of GDP measured in current US$. China's opening-up to long-term capital flows and export-led economic growth is clear from World Trade Organization (WTO) data. Over the past four years, China has been the largest exporter of goods in the world. The three most important export destinations are the United States, Japan, and South Korea, whose shares in Chinese exports are 21%, 10.3%, and 5.3%, respectively. The significance of foreign investors for the export value of Chinese goods is clear from the data on added value within the total value of gross exports from China. The leading export industry is computer and electronic production, with 23.8% of the total exports, of which domestic components account for 10.7% and foreign value added for 13.1%.[20] According to WTO data, between 1995 and 2011, China was the country with the fastest rate of growth of participation in global value chains (GVC), 18.6%, compared to average rates of 8% for the developed economies and 13.1% for the developing economies.

Unlike some of the small open economies amongst the fastest-growing economies in 2000–2014, in addition to this economic growth, China also saw its human development index rise significantly, up from 0.502 in 1990 to 0.591 in 2000 and 0.727 at the end of 2014.[21] So, in twenty-five years, China's HDI has gone up 44.8%, representing yet another major qualitative step forward: economic growth accompanied by economic development.

4.2 The Fastest-Growing Economies Among the Oil- and Gas-Producing Countries

As noted above, the other fastest-growing economies for 2000 to 2014 can be divided between those whose accelerated growth was largely based on investment in energy (oil and natural gas production) and on related export revenues and those that based their growth on accelerated integration into global financial and trade flows and not primarily the energy sector.

4.2.1 Azerbaijan

In the first fourteen years of this century, Azerbaijan was the fastest-growing economy in the world. It succeeded in improving its relative economic position (Cg) by 212%. Looked at in terms of five-year periods, Azerbaijan achieved its greatest rate of growth and percentage boost in the Cg between 2000 and 2005 (an increase of 66.6%) and 2005 to 2009 (an increase of 81.8%). In 2009–2014, its relative economic standing improved by just a further 3%. Overall from 1990 to 2014 its Cg rose 42.1%, placing it 38th in the world in terms of rates of relative economic growth. This was at least partly due to the fact that the Azerbaijani economy's absolute and relative decline during 1990–2000 had placed it amongst the ten countries with the largest fall in relative economic standing during that period.

Azerbaijan's main export is oil. Its rising price was the most important variable underlying the high rates of GDP per capita growth during 2001–2010. The degree of financial liberalization and of financial globalization attained were not leading factors in its economic growth or its changing economic standing. The normalized values for the Chinn-Ito index ranged from 16.39 to a peak of 57.1.[22] During the periods of most impressive growth (2000–2005 and 2005–2009), a greater degree of de jure financial openness in 2002–2003 was followed by repression in 2004–2006, only to grow again over the following three years, which corresponded with accelerated economic growth. Even when de jure financial openness was growing (2007–2008), however, the main additional stimulus to growth came from changing oil prices on international markets, up on US markets from approximately US$75 per barrel in mid July 2007 to approximately US$147 per barrel a year later.

The government of Azerbaijan founded the State Oil Fund (SOFAZ – in 1999) and also owns the State Oil Company (SOCAR). According to WTO data, oil and gas sales account for 94.2% of all exports.[23] Taking place as it did during the first fourteen years of this century and after a major decline in the last decade of the twentieth century, Azerbaijan's economic growth was almost entirely related to investment projects in the energy sector, including the development of infrastructure to support the sector. Given that Azerbaijan does not publish an International Investment Position, we may use the data on net FDI from the World Bank database as a measure of de facto financial openness. According to this source, total net FDI inflows to Azerbaijan were US$12.94 billion between 2001 and 2005, US$19.32 billion between 2006 and 2010, and US$16.83 billion between 2011 and 2014.[24] According to UNCTAD data, the total FDI stock to GDP ratio was 16.2% in 2012 and 24.5% in 2014.[25] The country's external debt increased from US$1.52 billion in 2000 to US$11.69 billion in 2014 (669%). Nominal GDP was up from US$5.27 billion to US$75.2 billion (by 1,327%). These trends led to Azerbaijan abating its external debt to GDP ratio from 28.9% in 2000 to 15.5% in 2014. Between 2009 and 2014, external debt nonetheless increased by a factor of 2.5, while nominal GDP increased by a factor of only 1.7. Export revenues fell 3% during 2013 and were down 11% in 2014, as a result of the sharp fall in the price of its major export products. This country's financial opening-up has been gradual and, according to available data, the most important foreign investor has been the Russian Federation.

4.2.2 *Turkmenistan*

Turkmenistan was the fourth fastest-growing economy in the world in 2000–2014, improving its relative economic standing (Cg) by 129.7%. During the first five years of that period, Turkmenistan's growth was relatively modest, ranking just 50th in terms of Cg growth. Faster growth came between 2005 and 2014, with relative growth of 39.6% from 2005 to 2009 and 46.7% between 2009 and 2014. The economy also achieved an impressive reduction in its external debt to GDP ratio from 86.4% in 2000 to 0.9% to 2014, thanks to a fall in external debt from US$2.51 billion to US$0.44 billion and a simultaneous rise in nominal GDP from US$2.91 billion to US$47.93 billion.[26]

Its Chinn-Ito index score for the fourteen years to 2014 classifies Turkmenistan as a financially repressed economy in which financial liberalization largely related to attracting FDI to speed up natural gas and oil exploitation, the two main sources of its fast economic expansion (the normalized Ka_open value ranged between 0 and 16.38).[27] Like Azerbaijan, the Turkmen government does not publish its International Investment Position. According to the available data from the World Bank and UNCTAD, FDI inflows were strongest during precisely the two subperiods that Turkmenistan saw rapid economic growth. It was, moreover, largely due to flows of foreign capital from China, the Russian Federation, and Kazakhstan that it was able to expand production of natural gas and oil. According to World Bank data, net FDI inflows to Turkmenistan were US$7.84 billion in 2005–2009 and US$16.4 billion in 2010–2014.[28] UNCTAD data on net FDI does not differ significantly from the World Bank data, showing an improvement in the FDI stock to GDP ratio from something less than 20% in 2000 to 54.7% by the end of 2014.[29]

4.2.3 *Equatorial Guinea*

Equatorial Guinea has been the fastest-growing economy in the world for the past twenty-five years, boosting its relative economic standing by 2017% (percentage change in Cg). It was the fastest-growing economy in the ten years to 2000, when its Cg rose from 0.072 to 0.666 or by 817%. It was the discovery of off-shore oil wells that allowed this sudden growth in revenues based on oil and gas exports. Between 2000 and 2005, it was again the fastest-growing economy in the world, with Cg growth of 181.5%. World Bank data show net FDI inflows at

US$3.06 billion for these years. In the following four-year period (2005–2009), its relative economic growth fell 3.2%, even though net FDI inflows were still at US$2.56 billion (2008 was the only year with a net FDI outflow). Between 2009 and 2014, net FDI inflows increased to their highest level, US$10.57 billion.[30] In spite of still rising net FDI inflows nearly four times the level for the previous four-year period, falling oil and gas prices in 2013 and 2014 undermined further economic progress. Indeed, between 2009 and 2014, Equatorial Guinea was one of the worst performers in the world and its relative economic position fell 20.7%.

According to UNCTAD data (which is close to World Bank data for this country) its FDI stock to GDP ratio was up from 81.3% in 2012 to 120.6% in 2014.[31] The major foreign investors were from the United States, China, and France. The country does not provide national data through an International Investment Position, but in spite of its relative de jure financial closedness, with a Chinn-Ito index score of 0.1639 for 2000–2014 (Ka_open normalized value of 16.38),[32] the FDI stock to GDP ratio shows that it had attained a high level of de facto financial openness.

Equatorial Guinea's growth rates were very high between 1990 and 2005 (both relative rates as measured by the Cg and absolute as measured by GDP per capita), but the country has experienced economic backsliding in relative terms over the last ten years and in absolute terms since 2009. According to UNDP data, however, thanks to earlier growth the country has managed to transition from the group of undeveloped countries into the group of countries with medium human development (measured by HDI). In the 2000–2014, the country pushed up its HDI from 0.526 to 0.587 and life expectancy at birth is up from 48.2 in 1990 to 57.6 in 2014, which is undeniably significant progress. The increase in GNI per capita from US$1,207 to US$21,056[33] (by a factor of 17.4, measured in constant US$ from 2011 in PPP terms) shows that the major increase in revenues, after repatriation of their share by foreign investors to their countries of origin, has been distributed within a relatively narrow social layer.

Equatorial Guinea's de facto financial openness to foreign investment in the energy sector played a key role in achieving such high rates of economic growth from 1990 to 2005. The steep growth in its FDI stock to GDP ratio between 2009 and 2014 was, however, negatively correlated to actual growth rates. Equatorial Guinea based its attractiveness to FDI on its energy sector and rising oil and gas prices, and though the composition of FDI has shifted in recent years towards more intensive investment in infrastructural projects, the impact may not be felt in the short or even medium term.

4.2.4 *Mongolia*

From 2000 to 2014, Mongolia was the seventh fastest-growing economy in the world with a growth rate 105.8% faster than the world average. Like most countries in transition, it had suffered a sharp economic decline and steep deterioration in social conditions in the last decade of the twentieth century, due largely to the disintegration of the former Soviet Union, its major trading partner, and to deindustrialization. Nonetheless, Mongolia was the 22nd fastest-growing economy overall between 1990 and 2014, so that its rate of economic growth after 2000 was more than sufficient to compensate for the economic decline of the decade before. In terms of our analytical sub-periods, Mongolia was the 26th fastest-growing economy from 2000 to 2005, 31st from 2005 to 2009, and third fastest-growing economy from then to 2014.[34] This country is a typical example of the high positive correlation between intensive financial opening-up, particularly to FDI in the fuel and mining sectors (oil, gas, and gold), and sharply rising rates of economic growth. Mongolia is, moreover, representative of the pairing of rapidly increased external borrowing (in line with increasing FDI) and rising rates of economic growth (particularly during the last five years).

This intensive growth in de facto financial openness is clear from the data on its international investment position and its TOTAL measure for de facto financial openness. During the first five years of this century, Mongolia reduced its external debt/GDP ratio from 84.4% to 55.3%, only to see the indicator rise sharply between 2009 and 2014, from 65.1% to 173.3%. This was the sharpest rise in this indicator in any of 20 fastest-growing economies during this period. On the other hand, Mongolia's TOTAL measure had already reached 205.5% by 2010 and continued growing, to 254.4%, over the following four years.[35] The most important foreign direct investors in Mongolia include China, Canada, Russian Federation, the United States, and the United Kingdom. According to UNCTAD data, the cumulative stock of FDI into Mongolia was up from US$13.5 billion (in 2012) to US$16.7 billion (in 2014).[36] Mongolia's most important trading partner is China, whose markets account for nearly 90% of the country's exports. Export revenues are dominated by revenues from fuel and mining exports (83.7%).[37]

4.2.5 *Kazakhstan*

In the 2000–2014, Kazakhstan was the eighth fastest-growing economy in the world, improving its relative economic position by 98.1%. Like Mongolia, it faced major economic decline in ten years before that, due to the dissolution of the USSR, but the rates of growth achieved after 2000 have been sufficiently great for its relative economic standing to be 33.3% better than it was even in 1990. The level of de jure financial liberalization peaked in 2008 (the Chinn-Ito normalized index was 57.10), when the government of Kazakhstan reintroduced restrictions on short-term capital flows. Some of these measures were relaxed over the following three years, but the value of the index for 2011–2014 was down to 46.69.[38]

The key factors in this economic expansion were FDI inflows into the energy sector and export revenues thanks to rising oil and gas prices. According to WTO data, Kazakhstan's revenues from fuel and mining absolutely dominated its export revenues, accounting for 86.6%.[39] According to World Bank data, net FDI inflows to Kazakhstan between 2000 and 2014 totalled US$117.3 billion. The fastest period of relative economic growth was between 2000 and 2005, when the Cg rose 48.5%, it was the fifth fastest-growing economy in the world. It was 44th in 2005–2009 and 31st in 2009–2014. Net FDI inflows were US$14.2 billion, US$58.1 billion, and US$45.0 billion for those five-year periods respectively, but this has been followed by a declining rate of economic growth.

Unlike most of the other fastest-growing economies, portfolio investment has been a very significant source of financing for economic growth in Kazakhstan. According to US State Department data in the 2005–2015, total capital inflows based on portfolio investment were US$80.25 billion, of which equity portfolio investment accounted for US$11.84 billion and debt portfolio investment for US$68.41 billion.[40] The most important portfolio investors in Kazakhstan were the United States (average share 54%), the United Kingdom (7.2%), and Japan (7%). The main foreign investors through FDI were the United States, the Netherlands, France, and China. According to UNCTAD data, which does not differ significantly from World Bank data for Kazakhstan, the total amount of inward FDI in 2014 was US$124.7 billion. The FDI stock to GDP ratio for that year reached a level of 60.9%,[41] placing the country among the de facto financially open economies.

4.2.6 Angola

Between 2000 and 2014, Angola's relative economic standing improved by 85.5%, making it the 12th fastest-growing economy during that period overall. Its economic growth was (and remains) almost entirely dependent on oil production and oil prices, which account for 97.1% of export revenues.[42] Its absolute dependence on changes in oil prices is also clear from the data on relative rates of economic growth in the five-year sub-periods: Angola was the 19th fastest-growing economy with GDP per capita growth 27.1% faster than the world average in 2000–2005 and the third fastest with GDP per capita growth 47.2% faster over the four years to the end of 2009,[43] but only 113th, with a Cg fall of 0.9%, between 2009 and 2014, largely thanks to falling oil prices in 2013–2014.

Between 2000 and 2014, Angola's nominal GDP (in current prices and current US$) rose from US$9.13 billion to US$138.36 billion (jumping 89% in the period from 2009 to 2014 alone),[44] while its external debt rose from US$9.76 billion to US$28.45 billion. As a result, the external debt to GDP ratio fell from 106.9% to 20.6%. The population rose by nearly 54% during these fourteen years (101.6% during the last quarter century).[45] Thanks to its economic growth, Angola's HDI improved significantly, from 0.390 in 2000 to 0.532 in 2014.[46] Its rapid economic growth has not, however, been matched by a more balanced distribution of wealth, so that its IHDI (inequality-adjusted human development index) placed it eight places lower than its HDI ranking.[47] In any case, both criteria place it among the countries with low human development indices.

Angola's de jure financial openness is low. The normalized value of the Chinn-Ito index (Ka_open) for 1996–2006 was 16.39, while for 2007–2014 it was zero (because of measures introduced to restrict capital flows).[48] As is the case with most rapidly growing developing countries, the value of its Chinn-Ito index might lead one to suppose it is closed to foreign capital, but World Bank data on net FDI inflows show that Angola was fertile soil for profits. This has not just been a matter of transferring profits back to the investing country, but actually of using FDI in Angola itself as a type of platform for financing companies from the countries from which investment into plant and infrastructure to support oil exploitation was financed. According to the World Bank database, total net

FDI inflows to Angola were US$1.9 billion between 1991 and 1995, but US$5.1 billion in the next five years, and US$7.5 billion in 2001 to 2005. Over the following nine years to 2014, however, FDI flows reveal a net outflow of capital totalling some US$15.5 billion, 98 percent of this in 2011–2014.[49] These net FDI outflows were US$1.05 billion greater than earlier inflows and the most important factor in explaining Angola's relative falling behind average world GDP per capita growth in 2009–2014 and the consequent steep fall in its ranking as a fast-growing economy.

4.2.7 *Armenia, Belarus, and Uzbekistan*

In this group of countries from the 20 fastest-growing economies export revenues from oil and gas play a very significant role but do not dominate it as they did for the last six (not including China).

Armenia was the fifth fastest-growing economy in the world in 2000–2014, but the growth rate has been falling off. From 2000 to 2004, it was the second fastest-growing economy with Cg growth of 67.4%,[50] but over the following four-years a declining growth rate relegated it to 37th place, falling to 40th place by 2014. Fossil fuel exports accounted for nearly 38% of total revenue from exports, while parts for manufacturing made up another 27%.[51] Declining growth rates and rapid growth in external borrowing pushed up the external debt/GDP ratio from 52.8% in 2000 to 73.4% at the end of 2014. The external debt had increased by a factor of 8.5, nominal GDP by a factor of 6.1. There was a particularly marked imbalance between growth in the external debt and in nominal GDP during 2009–2014. The former rose 73.3%, the latter only 34.6%.[52] The country's International Investment Position shows a total value for gross capital flows of US$14.2 billion in 2010, with total assets at US$4.4 billion and total liabilities at US$9.8 billion. Four years later (2014), total assets had dropped to US$4.2 billion, while total liabilities were up to US$12.1 billion. As a result of such trends, the TOTAL score was 153.4% for 2010 but 139.9% for 2014.[53] This faster growth of external borrowing meant rising debt to non-residents, expressed in a negative NIIP to GDP, which rose from (–56.5%) to (–67.8) between 2010 and 2014. Accelerated de facto financial integration is indicated both by strong growth in the negative NIIP and the rising addiction to imported capital. In 2001, the NIIP was just US$(–1.43) billion, while by the end of 2007 it was US$(–2.09) billion, and seven years later US$(–7.89) billion.

Like Armenia, Belarus and Uzbekistan both saw rapid economic growth thanks to a significant boost from oil, gas and mineral exports, which accounted for at least 34% of all export revenues in both countries. A breakdown of Belarus' total export revenues reveals that manufacturing (primarily machinery) accounts for 45.7%, while oil and gas account for 34.1% of revenue.[54] During the first fourteen years of the century, Belarus saw its external debt rise from US$2.6 billion to US$40 billion (by 1437%), while nominal GDP went up from US$12.7 billion to US$76.1 billion (by 498%). The external debt/GDP ratio thus increased from 20.4% to 52.6%.[55] Belarus' main trading partners are Russia, the United Kingdom and Cyprus. According to World Bank data, cumulative net FDI inflows during the five years to 2005 were just US$1 billion. In the next five years they were US$7.62 billion and in the 2011–2014 they were US$9.57 billion. The country's Ka_open normalized value indicates de jure closure to capital flows, but its TOTAL score suggests an economic growth rate largely due to sharply increasing imports of capital as FDI and foreign loans (in addition to higher export revenues from oil and gas and specific "geographic rent"). The TOTAL score was up from 144.6% in 2000 to 426.4% in 2014.[56] In other words, de facto financial openness practically tripled during the first fourteen years of this century. The largest inflow of capital to Belarus came from Russia, its most significant political and economic partner.

Between 2000 and 2014, Uzbekistan was the 15th fastest-growing economy, with GDP per capita growing 79.2% faster than the world average. According to WTO data, the country's export revenues came largely from fuels and mining (44.6%), approximately equal to the combined share of revenues from manufacturing and agriculture.[57] Unlike Belarus, Uzbekistan's external borrowing, as measured by the external debt to GDP ratio, fell significantly: from 36.2% in 2000 to 21.4% in 2014. The normalized value of the Ka_open for the first fourteen years of this century ranged from 0 to 16.48, indicating relative de jure financial closure.[58] According to UNCTAD and Santander Group data, however, Uzbekistan's FDI capital stock rose from US$7.6 billion in 2012 to US$9 billion in 2014.[59] That was partly thanks to the country's redefinition of its legislative framework for FDI and major contracts agreed with South Korea in 2011 (US$2.6 billion), China (over US$5 billion in infrastructure) in 2014, and Japan in 2015 (US$5 billion in the energy sector). So, while the country was de jure a financially repressed economy, de facto it secured major sources of growth through revenues from energy and infrastructural projects to support investment in that and related sectors (including chemicals), largely by being financially open to FDI-based inward flows of capital. The country's strategic economic interests are almost exclusively linked to capital flows from the East, or more precisely the Far East.

4.2.8 The Fastest-Growing Poor Economies

Ethiopia, Cambodia, Chad, Tajikistan, Lao PDR, and Bhutan were all among the 20 fastest-growing economies in 2000–2014, with Cg rises of 91.3%, 88.2%, 78.6%, 77.8%, 76.2%, and 73.3%, respectively. Except Chad, none of them based their economic growth on prospective energy resources so much as on speeding-up integration into international capital flows thanks to the availability of cheap labour, favourable conditions for producing parts (manufacturing) or agricultural production in certain sub-regions (e.g. Ethiopia), financial resources approved as government aid (e.g. Ethiopia again), and China's growing interest in developing its influence in Africa, parts of the former Soviet Union, and southern Asia.

Between 2000 and 2014, Ethiopia's nominal GDP was up 575% and its external debt was up 201%. This brought its external debt to GDP ratio down from 66.8% to 29.8%.[60] Success in attracting foreign investors, especially from China, means its FDI stock has gone up from US$5.1 billion (in 2012) to US$7.3 billion (in 2014). The FDI stock to GDP ratio is still low (13.9%), but strategic partners' growing interest in investing and aid resources (US$3.1 billion) have facilitated more rapid economic growth, boosting the human development index over the past fourteen years from 0.284 to 0.442. The IHDI for 2014 was, however, 0.312, suggesting significant inequality in allocation of the country's growing revenues. In spite of high rates of economic growth, Ethiopia is still one of the ten poorest countries in the world. Results over the fourteen years to 2014 have been significant, but Ethiopia's GDP per capita in 2000 was only 2% of the world average (a Cg of 0.020). This gap has been significantly reduced, but in 2014 GDP per capita was still just 4% of the world average.[61] The country would need double-digit rates of growth for ten years to see results of the sort achieved by China and India in the 1990s.

Like Ethiopia, Cambodia has managed to reduce its external debt to GDP ratio significantly: from 72.5% in 2000 to 40.6% in 2014. According to WTO data, Cambodia's trade to GDP ratio was 137.5% in 2014, reflecting a relatively high degree of trade openness. Export expansion has been the key factor in more rapid economic growth. The country's main trading partners are the EU (27.2%), the United States (23.5%), and Hong Kong (17.2%). Manufacturing dominates exports (92.8%), with agriculture accounting for only 7% of total export revenue.[62] According to UNCTAD, FDI stock had reached US$13.1 billion by 2014, with foreign investors from China taking the lead.[63]

Chad is the only country from this group whose attractiveness for FDI is largely based on the exploitation of oil and other energy resources. While it ranked very low in the World Bank's *Doing Business*,[64] foreign investors (from Nigeria, France, the United Kingdom) are showing increasing interest in investing there. Like other economies from this group discussed above, Chad has managed to reduce its external debt to GDP ratio significantly – from 79.5% in 2000 to 20.5% in 2014. Total FDI stock is up from US$4.4 billion (in 2012) to US$5.5 billion (in 2014), which is to say from 34.1% to 39.6% of GDP.[65] According to World Bank data, the country's nominal GDP has risen tenfold over the past fourteen years, while the trade openness achieved over the past four years, as measured by the trade to GDP ratio, is now 85.2%, reflecting increasing trade liberalization.

Between 2000 and 2014, Tajikistan and Lao brought their external debt to GDP ratios down from 132.5% to 43.8% and from 146.5% to 89.4%, respectively. At the same time, Bhutan practically doubled its external borrowing from 48.3% to 93.9% of GDP. According to World Bank data, during this period Tajikistan's nominal GDP increased by a factor of 10.7, that of Lao by a factor of 6.9. Tajikistan's main export products were aluminium and silk and its main trading partners Turkey, China, and Kazakhstan.[66] Bhutan owes its economic growth over the preceding period primarily to the intense economic growth of the second most populous and 14th fastest-growing economy in the world, India, to which it exports 93.7% of all its products (the dominant sectors: manufacturing and fuels and mining).

4.2.9 India

Unlike China, which successfully tackled its birth rate issue three decades ago, India is still experiencing high rates of population growth. The population rose 47.8% over the last twenty-five years, 23% during the first fourteen years of this century alone.[67] In spite of these high rates of population growth, India was also the eighth fastest-growing economy in the world in 1990–2014, with Cg growth of 126.7%, though only the 14th fastest-growing economy during 2000–2014, with a Cg percentage increase of 81.8%. In the 2000–2014, nominal GDP increased by 330% and the external debt by 360%, so that the external debt to GDP ratio has remained relatively stable, up from 21.2% in 2000 to 22.6% in 2014.[68] According to WTO data for the last three years, the trade to GDP ratio average value was 53.6%. Again, unlike China, India had a merchandise trade deficit through the entire period. In 2014, the deficit was US$141.6 billion. Exports of goods broke down sectorally as follows: manufacturing (62.3%), fuels and mining (23.3%), and agriculture (13.5%).[69] On the other hand, India ran a surplus in services and it is in this area that the country has proved itself one of the most dynamic and competitive economies of the past twenty-five years.

As to de jure financial openness, the normalized value of the Ka_open index of 16.48 for the entire period from 1990 to 2014 indicates how tightly de jure financial controls in India were and the degree of attention being directed towards capital flows, particularly short-term ones. On the other hand, the TOTAL score suggests a gradual increase in de facto openness – up from 41.3% in 2002 to 67% in 2009, but falling slightly to 65.5% in 2014.[70] Figure 4.4 shows the difference in cumulative net inward FDI to India and Brazil (according to the World Bank methodology) for the following periods: 1981–1990, 1991–2000, 2001–2010, and 2011–2014. Even though the amount for India for the entire period from 1991 to 2014 was approximately equal to the amount received by Brazil in just the last four years (2011–2014), the impact of the FDI on economic growth has been significantly greater in India than in Brazil. In the 2009–2014, Brazil was growing at a rate 3.6% faster than the world average, but India was outstripping it by as much as 23.2%. In the 2000–2014, Brazil's relative growth, measured by percentage change in the Cg, was 12%, making it the 91st fastest-growing economy in the world. India's Cg was up 81.8%, placing it 14th.

In making this comparison, however, one must bear in mind the different starting positions and Cg values for these two countries. In the final year covered by our analysis (2014), GDP per capita in Brazil was 74.8% of the world average (its Cg was 0.748). Even after twenty-five years of significant growth, India's GDP per capita was still only 15.8% of the world average (its Cg was 0.158) in 2014. Nonetheless, the fact that capital inflows based on inward FDI were almost three times higher for

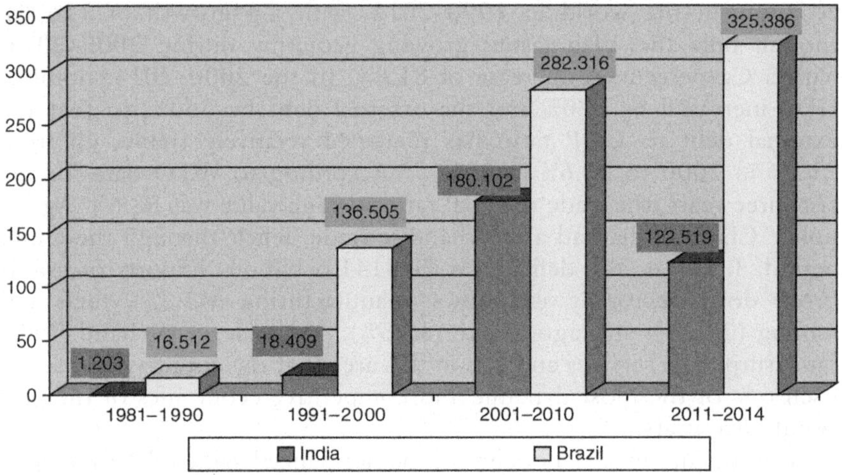

Fig. 4.4 Total net FDI inflows to India and Brazil: 1980–2014 cumulative amounts for the periods: 1981–1990, 1991–2000, 2001–2010, and 2011–2014 – in billions of current US$

Source: The World Bank database

Brazil than for India, but India's rate of growth exceeded the world average rate of growth by 6.4 times the amount Brazil's did, shows how much less efficient each unit of inward FDI into Brazil was than units invested in India between 2009 and 2014. At the beginning of this section we looked at the data on net FDI inflows to China, one of the most important destinations for FDI in the world between 2000 and 2014. According to the most recent data for 2015 (a year not included in our time series for the analysis of growth rates), India captured the top position in the world as a destination for manufacturing-oriented FDI.[71]

The country's strategy is focused on attracting as many manufacturing-oriented foreign investors as possible with a view both to reducing the trade deficit and to accelerating investment in infrastructure, which is considerably less developed than in China, while at the same time maintaining a positive balance of trade in services. So, while the two most populous countries in the world have taken different approaches to promoting economic growth over the past twenty-five years, both economies have followed policies of controlled and gradual liberalization of capital flows, combined with trade liberalization. High levels of supply on a very competitive labour market at a price that is a fraction of that in the developed countries of the West, whether for semiskilled or the most highly skilled labour, and the size and potential of these two countries' markets have proved attractive to foreign investors, on the one hand, while also allowing a select group of domestic companies to become world leaders or at least to join the upper echelons, on the other.

Notes

1. See Chapter 2.
2. Source: The Chinn-Ito Index is available at http://web.pdx.edu/~ito/kaopen_2014.xls. It has two values, the Kaopen which for China was (-1.18766), and the Ka_open, whose value is given in the text.
3. For data on the US$/CNY exchange rate, see http://www.tradingeconomics.com/china/currency
4. Source: The Government of the People's Republic of China: http://www.safe.gov.cn/wps/wcm/connect/11518a004f5a09699f869f219f90791c/IIP.xls?MOD=AJPERES&CACHEID=11518a004f5a09699f869f219f90791c (accessed on 12 May 2016).
5. Source: Chinability – http://www.chinability.com/Reserves.htm (accessed on 20 May 2016).
6. Source: the World Bank – http://data.worldbank.org/indicator/DT.DOD.DECT.CD (accessed on 19 May 2016).
7. Sources: the World Bank database for China's GDP; China's International investment position taken from: http://www.safe.gov.cn/wps/wcm/connect/11518a004f5a09699f869f219f90791c/IIP.xls?MOD=AJPERES&CACHEID=11518a004f5a09699f869f219f90791c
8. Source: The World Bank database – http://data.worldbank.org/indicator/BX.KLT.DINV.CD.WD?page=1
9. The author's calculations, based on World Bank data.
10. For China's International Investment Position see: http://www.safe.gov.cn/wps/wcm/connect/11518a004f5a09699f869f219f90791c/IIP.xls?MOD=AJPERES&CACHEID=11518a004f5a09699f869f219f90791c
11. UNCTAD FDI statistics are based on the *Balance of Payments Statistics – Manual Five of the IMF*, while the World Bank data are based on the *Balance of Payments Statistics – Manual Six of the IMF*. The difference between them is due to item three in *BOP Manual Six*, which includes the items contained in *BOP Manual Five* plus investment between fellow enterprises. The author requested clarification from World Bank staff on these differences and

received an answer on 22 June 2016 in an email officially registered under the number: 17607-Data, Development Data Group, the World Bank.

12. See: US Department of State 2015a, available at: http://www.state.gov/documents/organization/241728.pdf (accessed on 24 May 2016)
13. Source: Banks around the World – http://www.relbanks.com/worlds-top-banks/assets
14. DBS Group Research 2015 https://webcache.googleusercontent.com/search?q=cache:GBNQJ9dlur8J:https://www.dbs.com.sg/treasures/aics/pdfController.page%3Fpdfpath%3D/content/article/pdf/AIO/150707_insights_sector_reforms_to_boost_china_banks.pdf+&cd=7&hl=en&ct=clnk&gl=ba
15. Source: DBS Group Research 2015, p. 12.
16. Bloomberg – http://www.bloomberg.com/news/articles/2015-10-23/china-takes-riskiest-step-by-scrapping-deposit-rate-controls
17. Source: IMF – http://www.imf.org/external/pubs/ft/survey/so/2015/new120115a.htm
18. Source: Bloomberg – http://www.bloomberg.com/quote/SHSZ300:IND
19. See: Chinability – http://www.chinability.com/Reserves.htm
20. Data on China's international trade presented in this paragraph are taken from the WTO database: https://www.wto.org/english/res_e/statis_e/miwi_e/CN_e.pdf
21. See: http://CountryEconomy.com – http://countryeconomy.com/hdi/china
22. See: The Chinn-Ito index at: http://web.pdx.edu/~ito/kaopen_2014.xls
23. Source: The World Trade Organization – http://stat.wto.org/CountryProfile/WSDBCountryPFView.aspx?Language=E&Country=AZ
24. The World Bank – http://data.worldbank.org/indicator/BX.KLT.DINV.CD.WD?page=1
25. See: https://en.portal.santandertrade.com/establish-overseas/azerbaijan/investing
26. The World Bank – http://data.worldbank.org/indicator/BX.KLT.DINV.CD.WD?page=1
27. Source: http://web.pdx.edu/~ito/kaopen_2014.xls
28. The World Bank – http://data.worldbank.org/indicator/BX.KLT.DINV.CD.WD?page=1
29. Banco Santander – https://en.portal.santandertrade.com/establish-overseas/turkmenistan/investing-3
30. The World Bank database – http://data.worldbank.org/indicator/BX.KLT.DINV.CD.WD?page=1
31. UNCTAD data are used in the Banco Santander report on investing in Equatorial Guinea – https://en.portal.santandertrade.com/establish-overseas/equatorial-guinea/investing-3

32. Chinn-Ito database: http://web.pdx.edu/~ito/kaopen_2014.xls
33. Data on HDI and GNI per capita are taken from *UNDP Human Development Report – Briefing note for Equatorial Guinea* available at: http://hdr.undp.org/sites/all/themes/hdr_theme/country-notes/GNQ.pdf
34. The author's calculations based on the World Bank database.
35. Source: The author's calculation based on data of the National Bank of Mongolia – available at: https://www.mongolbank.mn/eng/liststatistic.aspx?id=4_2
36. See: https://en.portal.santandertrade.com/establish-overseas/mongolia/investing-3
37. Source: The World Trade Organization.
38. Source:http://web.pdx.edu/~ito/kaopen_2014.xls
39. World Trade Organization: http://stat.wto.org/CountryProfile/WSDBCountryPFView.aspx?Language=E&Country=KZ
40. US Department of State 2015b, p. 28, available at: http://www.state.gov/documents/organization/241825.pdf
41. UNCTAD data for Kazakhstan presented in the Banco Santander report available at: https://en.portal.santandertrade.com/establish-overseas/kazakhstan/investing
42. Source WTO – available at: http://stat.wto.org/CountryProfile/WSDBCountryPFView.aspx?Language=E&Country=AO
43. The percentages given for Angola's faster rates of GDP per capita growth are based on percentage changes in Angola's growth coefficient (Cg). That is, the percentages by which Angola is faster than world average GDP per capita growth during the two periods in question represent percentage changes in the Cg, which were calculated by the author using the World Bank database.
44. The source of the data for nominal GDP is the World Bank database.
45. Source:https://www.google.ba/?gws_rd=cr,ssl&ei=ywJcV58Kh-JRqc-F0As#q=population+angola
46. Source: UNDP – available at: http://hdr.undp.org/en/composite/trends
47. Source: UNDP – available at: http://hdr.undp.org/en/composite/IHDI
48. Source:http://web.pdx.edu/~ito/kaopen_2014.xls
49. Source: The World Bank database – http://data.worldbank.org/indicator/BX.KLT.DINV.CD.WD?page=1
50. The author's calculation based on the World Bank database.
51. Source: The World Trade Organization – available at: http://stat.wto.org/CountryProfile/WSDBCountryPFView.aspx?Language=E&Country=AM
52. Source: The World Bank
53. Source: IMF – available at: http://dsbb.imf.org/Pages/SDDS/InterInvPos.aspx
54. Source: The World Trade Organisation – available at: http://stat.wto.org/CountryProfile/WSDBCountryPFView.aspx?Language=E&Country=BY

55. Source: The World Bank database – http://data.worldbank.org/indicator/NY.GDP.MKTP.CD?view=chart
56. Source: Calculated by the author using data published by the National Bank of the Republic of Belarus – available at: http://www.nbrb.by/engl/statistics/InvestPos/Quarterly6/
57. Source: The World Trade Organization – available at: http://stat.wto.org/CountryProfile/WSDBCountryPFView.aspx?Language=E&Country=UZ
58. Available at: http://web.pdx.edu/~ito/kaopen_2014.xls
59. See at: https://en.portal.santandertrade.com/establish-overseas/uzbekistan/investing
60. Source: The World Bank.
61. The author's calculations, based on the World Bank database.
62. The World Trade Organization – available at: http://stat.wto.org/CountryProfile/WSDBCountryPFView.aspx?Language=E&Country=KH
63. See at: https://en.portal.santandertrade.com/establish-overseas/cambodia/investing-3
64. The World Bank 2015a, p. 178; available at: http://www.doingbusiness.org/~/media/GIAWB/Doing%20Business/Documents/Annual-Reports/English/DB15-Full-Report.pdf
65. See at: https://en.portal.santandertrade.com/establish-overseas/chad/investing-3
66. See: The World Bank 2015b, available at: https://www.worldbank.org/content/dam/Worldbank/Publications/ECA/centralasia/Tajikistan-Economic-Update-Spring-2015-en.pdf
67. See at: http://www.worldometers.info/world-population/india-population/
68. The author's calculations, based on the World Bank database.
69. Source: The World Trade Organization – available at: http://stat.wto.org/CountryProfile/WSDBCountryPFView.aspx?Language=E&Country=IN
70. The author's calculations, using data from the Reserve Bank of India available at: https://rbi.org.in/scripts/BS_PressReleaseDisplay.aspx?prid=33593
71. See: The Diplomat, "India Takes Over from China as Top Global FDI Destination in 2015". Available at: http://thediplomat.com/2016/04/india-takes-over-from-china-as-top-global-fdi-destination-in-2015/

References

Deutsche Bank - DBS Group Research, China Banking Sector. (7 July 2015). https://webcache.googleusercontent.com/search?q=cache:GBNQJ9dlur8J:https://www.dbs.com.sg/treasures/aics/pdfController.page%3Fpdfpath%

3D/content/article/pdf/AIO/150707_insights_sector_reforms_to_boost_china_banks.pdf±&cd=7&hl=en&ct=clnk&gl=ba

The Chinn-Ito Index database. http://web.pdx.edu/~ito/Chinn-Ito_website.htm and http://web.pdx.edu/~ito/kaopen_2014.xls

The Diplomat. India takes over from China as top global FDI Destination in 2015. http://thediplomat.com/2016/04/india-takes-over-from-china-as-top-global-fdi-destination-in-2015/

The World Bank. (2015a). *Doing business 2015 – going beyond efficiency*. Washington. http://www.doingbusiness.org/~/media/GIAWB/Doing%20Business/Documents/Annual-Reports/English/DB15-Full-Report.pdf

The World Bank. (2015b). *Tajikistan – slowing growth, rising uncertainties, Tajikistan economic update No.1*. Spring 2015. https://www.worldbank.org/content/dam/Worldbank/Publications/ECA/centralasia/Tajikistan-Economic-Update-Spring-2015-en.pdf

US Department of State. (2015a). *2015 investment climate statement – China*. Washington. May 2015. http://www.state.gov/documents/organization/241728.pdf

US Department of State. (2015b). *Kazakhstan investment climate statement 2015*. Washington. May 2015. http://www.state.gov/documents/organization/241825.pdf

Websites

Banco Santander:

https://en.portal.santandertrade.com/establish-overseas/azerbaijan/investing

https://en.portal.santandertrade.com/establish-overseas/kazakhstan/investing

https://en.portal.santandertrade.com/establish-overseas/mongolia/investing-3

Bloomberg:

http://www.bloomberg.com/news/articles/2015-10-23/china-takes-riskiest-step-by-scrapping-deposit-rate-controls

http://www.bloomberg.com/quote/SHSZ300:IND

Chinability: http://www.chinability.com/Reserves.htm

CountryEconomy.com http://countryeconomy.com/hdi/china

National Bank of the Republic of Belarus: http://www.nbrb.by/engl/statistics/InvestPos/Quarterly6/

People's Bank of China:

http://www.safe.gov.cn/wps/wcm/connect/11518a004f5a09699f869f219f90791c/IIP.xls?MOD=AJPERES&CACHEID=11518a004f5a09699f869f219f90791c

The Government of the People's Republic of China:
http://www.safe.gov.cn/wps/wcm/connect/11518a004f5a09699f869f219f90791c/IIP.xls?MOD=AJPERES&CACHEID=11518a004f5a09699f869f219f90791c
The National Bank of Mongolia: https://www.mongolbank.mn/eng/liststatistic.aspx?id=4_2
The Reserve Bank of India available at: https://rbi.org.in/scripts/BS_PressReleaseDisplay.aspx?prid=33593

The World Bank:
http://data.worldbank.org/indicator/DT.DOD.DECT.CD
http://data.worldbank.org/indicator/NY.GDP.MKTP.CD?view=chart
http://data.worldbank.org/indicator/BX.KLT.DINV.CD.WD?page=1

The World Trade Organization:
http://stat.wto.org/CountryProfile/WSDBCountryPFView.aspx?Language=E&Country=AM
http://stat.wto.org/CountryProfile/WSDBCountryPFView.aspx?Language=E&Country=AO
http://stat.wto.org/CountryProfile/WSDBCountryPFView.aspx?Language=E&Country=BY
http://stat.wto.org/CountryProfile/WSDBCountryPFView.aspx?Language=E&Country=IN
http://stat.wto.org/CountryProfile/WSDBCountryPFView.aspx?Language=E&Country=KH
http://stat.wto.org/CountryProfile/WSDBCountryPFView.aspx?Language=E&Country=KZ
http://stat.wto.org/CountryProfile/WSDBCountryPFView.aspx?Language=E&Country=UZ

UNDP:
http://hdr.undp.org/en/composite/trends
http://hdr.undp.org/en/composite/IHDI
http://hdr.undp.org/sites/all/themes/hdr_theme/country-notes/GNQ.pdf

CHAPTER 5

Global Financial Openness in the Advanced, Emerging and Developing Countries: A Brief Overview

In the preceding chapter, we presented an analysis of actual rates of economic growth, changes in relative economic standing, and financial openness for practically all of the 20 fastest-growing economies in the world from 2000 to 2014. Eighteen of these countries were developing economies (including emerging markets), while just two were developed economies. The major changes in economic power then playing out across the world between the advanced and developing countries (for simplicity's sake, we will include "emerging economies" under "developing countries") are also reflected in the data on changes in their relative shares in world GDP creation.

According to World Bank data, nominal world GDP (in current prices and current US$) rose from US$31.1 trillion to US$76.2 trillion over the first thirteen years of the century.[1] Data for the first thirteen years of the century are used here because of the availability of data on the international investment position both globally and by region, as published by the IMF in two publications in 2008 and 2015.[2] The advanced countries' nominal GDP during those thirteen years rose from US$25.8 trillion to US$45.3 trillion (by 75.5%), while that of developing countries rose from US$5.3 trillion to US$30.9 trillion (by 480%). Their relative shares in world GDP have thus changed considerably: falling significantly for the advanced countries and rising sharply for the developing countries.[3]

On the other hand, IMF data on total assets and liabilities, recorded in the International Investment Position report as part of the balance of

F. Čaušević, *A Study into Financial Globalization, Economic Growth and (In)Equality*, DOI 10.1007/978-3-319-51403-1_5

payments statistics, show total assets for all countries in the world in 2001 at US$30.7 trillion, with total liabilities at US$32.2 trillion. That year, advanced countries' assets amounted to US$29.1 trillion and liabilities to US$29.3 trillion. By the end of 2013, total world assets were US$135.3 trillion and total liabilities US$135.3 billion. Advanced countries' total assets were $115.1 trillion and total liabilities $115.4 trillion. Developing countries' assets rose between 2001 to 2013 from US$1.6 trillion to US$20.3 trillion, while liabilities rose from US$2.9 trillion to US$19.9 trillion.[4]

Naturally enough, China and India both played a special role in this increasing significance of developing economies, the rise in their GDP and the sharp increase in their share in world GDP creation. On the other hand, some of the other most populous developing countries, like Brazil and Mexico, were also becoming very important destinations for international capital flows. Their models of economic growth, however, differed considerably from those pursued by China, South-East Asia, and India. Brazil and Mexico recorded steep growth in their negative NIIP. During the first seven years of the century, Brazil's total assets rose from US$107 billion to US$370 billion, but total liabilities went up from US$372 billion to US$979 billion. Similarly, Mexico's assets increased from US$106 billion to US$218 billion, as total liabilities rose from US$355 billion to US$612 billion. By comparison, China's total assets went up from US$930 billion to US$2,288 billion, while total liabilities grew from US$637 billion to US$1,266 billion in just the four years from 2004 to 2007. By the end of 2007, the Taiwan Province of China's total assets were US$850 billion and its total liabilities just US$383 billion. Hong Kong, like mainland China and Taiwan, also belonged to the economies with a net positive international investment position (net capital-exporting economies).[5]

Using the available IMF data on the IIP and World Bank data on nominal GDP for the relevant years (2001, 2007 and 2013), one can derive values for the TOTAL measure of de facto financial openness. The resulting measures allow us to conclude that both advanced and developing countries saw significant increases in de facto financial openness, but the trajectories of the international capital flows and the degree to which they were used to stimulate economic growth reveal a major disparity between the total sum of international capital flows to the advanced countries and that available to the developing countries, particularly in comparison to their relative contributions to world GDP growth.

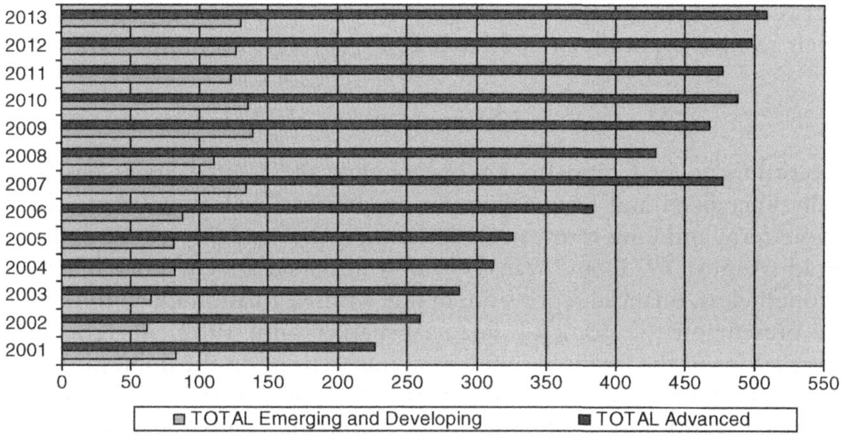

Fig. 5.1 TOTAL measure of financial openness: (assets+liabilities)/GDP for the advanced and developing countries –2001–2013 (in percentages)

Source: Prepared by the author using calculations based on IMF and World Bank data (sources cited in the endnote number 137)

Figure 5.1 illustrates this major disproportion in levels of "financial globalisation", expressed as the ratio of accumulated stocks of total assets and total liabilities to GDP. The overall level of de facto financial openness in the world rose from 201% in 2001 to 374% in 2007, to reach 355% by the end of 2013. The advanced countries' TOTAL measure of financial openness went up from 227% in 2001 to 477% in 2007 and 509% in 2013. This intensive opening up largely to FDI-based inflows of foreign capital has also increased developing countries' de facto financial openness, albeit to a rather lower level. In 2001, the developing countries' TOTAL measure was 83%. It was 134% six years later and 130% in 2013. Clearly, the ratio of accumulated stocks of assets and liabilities to GDP has been growing faster for the advanced countries than for developing countries.

The value of TOTAL measure rose by 124% in advanced countries, compared to 57% in developing countries. The absolute value of accumulated stocks of capital is an even better indicator of this disproportion in the concentration of international capital flows. Even if the disproportion in the concentration of overall stocks of capital reduced between 2000 and 2013, the disparity between the concentration of capital flows and share in world GDP creation indicates that the rising values of capital flows between advanced countries were not positively correlated to changes in their relative or, between 2007 and 2009, absolute economic standing.

5.1 The United States of America

According to its Chinn-Ito Ka_open index, the United States has been fully liberalized and financially open to international capital flows, both short-term and long-term, since declaring inconvertibility of the dollar to gold (August 1971) and transition to a free float system (March 1973). Nonetheless, financial repression, in line with Regulation Q, continued to be present on the domestic financial market until 1982. All remaining restrictions to the freedom of financial transactions on the domestic financial market imposed previously by the US government were abolished between 1980 and 1986, the most important being the interest rate ceilings for bank deposits imposed in 1934 (by the FDR Government) and only done away within 1982 (interest-rate deregulation). Thanks to such measures of financial liberalization of the domestic market, US financial markets had by 1986 been entirely liberalized for both domestic and foreign transactions.

Measures of restrictive monetary policy (monetary targeting), conducted by the Fed between 1980 and 1982, led to deep recession and a sharp increase in unemployment rates, from under 5% in the late 1970s to 10.8% by the end of 1982. These trends, along with abolition of interest rate ceilings on deposits and loans, contributed to reducing the importance of US banks globally. This lessening in their importance during the 1980s was evident from the fact that the two largest of the ten largest banks in the world in 1981 came from the United States (Bank of America and Citicorp), while a mere seven years later, in 1988, the year Basel I was adopted, not one of the top ten did. That year, nine of them were from Japan and just one from Europe. This relative falling behind by US banks compared to Japanese ones (in the first instance) and even French ones was reflected in the fact that the assets of US banks in the top 300 only tripled between 1974 and 1988, while Japanese banks from the same group of 300 was their assets increase by a factor of 13.[6] On the other hand, the quality of Japanese banks' assets deteriorated sharply during the second half of the 1980s. US banks' assets did not.

During the final decade of the last century, but particularly between 1995 and 2000, the US economy saw marked expansion and a period of domination, particularly in the so-called new economy (TMT or technology-media-telecommunications). The growth of productivity in computer production from 1995 to 1999 was impressive – with average productivity growth of 41.7%.[7] The manufacturing sector achieved a rate of 4.58% during the same period, compared to just 2.58% for 1972 to 1995. Productivity growth in other sectors, like non-durables and non-computers, was not even close to that in computer manufacturing. This impressive productivity growth in computer manufacturing and the IT industry overall created overheated expectations amongst financial investors over the possibilities for rising share prices in the sector. Their "irrational exuberance" led to the dot-com bubble and its implosion. The period of greatest growth in TMT-sector share prices was between March 1999 and March 2000, when the NASDAQ went up 105%.[8]

During the first half of the 1980s faith in the US$ was restored largely on the basis of the capital flowing into the United States from abroad motivated by high real yields on Treasury bonds thanks to highly restrictive monetary policy. During the second half of the 1990s, the dollar's strengthening was due to inflows of FDI and net equity portfolio investment motivated by high yields on corporate sector shares associated with IT or TMT companies. That yields on such shares were largely driven by rising prices (capital gains) and considerably less by dividend growth is confirmed by data like that cited in the World Economic Outlook for 2001, namely that the Price to Earnings ratio for 1960–2000 was 16.2, but 33.4 for 1998–2000.[9]

The liberalization of US financial markets and free capital flows contributed to a sharp growth in total capital flows in both directions – in and out. According to Fed data on the International Investment Position (IIP), the ratio of total capital flows in both directions (assets+liabilities) to GDP or the TOTAL measure rose from 84.2% to 165.7% in the period from 1990 to 2000.[10] In absolute terms, gross capital flows in and out of the United States went up from US$4,981 billion to US$16,820 billion (237.7%), while nominal GDP went up from US$5,915 billion to US$10,148 billion (71.6%). During the same period, net capital flows into the United States as measured by the NIIP (Assets-Liabilities) increased from (-2.5%) to (–15.1%) of GDP. In other words, the increase in US nominal GDP between 1990 and 2000 was financed not just by domestic savings, but also by net imports of capital, which increased in relative terms by a factor of approximately 6. In absolute terms, net imports of capital into the United States went up by a factor of 10.3 (from US$149 billion to US$1,537 billion) (Figure 5.2).

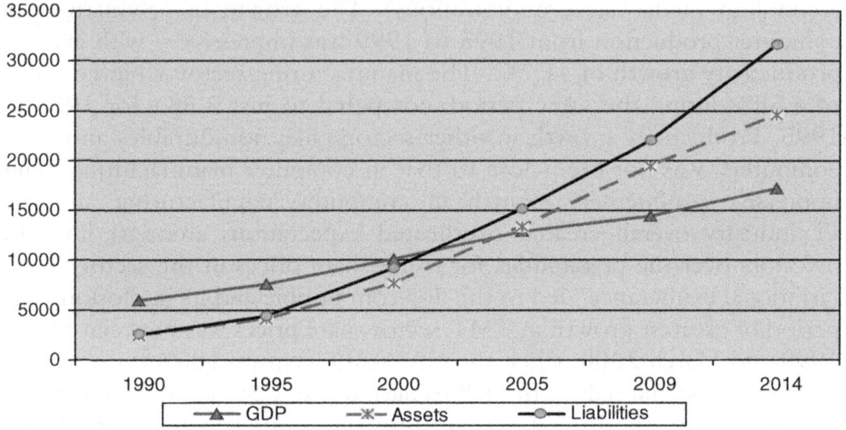

Fig. 5.2 The international investment position and GDP of the United States: 1990–2014

Source: The Federal Reserve Bank of St Louis – Economic Research https://research.stlouisfed.org/fred2/series/IIPUSASSA

In the nine years to 2009, US nominal GDP went up 42%, but total capital flows measured by the TOTAL measure rose from 166% to 288% of GDP. A further increase in nominal GDP of 19.2% over the period from recessionary 2009 to the end of 2014 was accompanied by a sharp increase in *net imports of capital* – from 18.2% to 40.9% of GDP. Such a hike in the import of capital over a period of just five years is unprecedented in post-war US history. Over this five-year post-recessionary period, US foreign liabilities rose US$9,561 billion, while US assets abroad increased $5,169 billion.[11]

5.2 Financial Openness and Economic Growth in the EU

In Chapter 3, which includes our analysis of rates of economic growth expressed in percentage change to the growth coefficient, we have already noted that EU countries can be divided into two subgroups on the basis of their results: the first subgroup comprises the EU-15 countries, which experienced negative changes to the Cg during the fourteen years to 2014 (that is they experienced lower or significantly lower GDP per capita growth rates than the world average), while the EU-13 countries (received into EU membership between 2004 and 2013) other than Malta and Cyprus have seen their relative economic standing improve, as expressed in higher values of the Cg for 2014 than for 2000.

Between 2000 and 2014, only six EU economies made the cut of the 50 fastest-growing economies: Latvia (20th), Romania (31st), Bulgaria (37th), Estonia (39th), the Slovak Republic (40th), and Poland (46th). The next 50 (from 51 to 100) contained only two EU economies: the Czech Republic (85th) and Hungary (94th). The only other two EU economies with a higher Cg in 2014 than in 2000 were Croatia (101st) and Slovenia (107th). This means that these 10 EU countries did manage to improve their relative economic standing in the world (i.e. saw Cg growth). Their GDP per capita growth rates were higher than the world average. Changes in the growth coefficient range from 3.9% for Slovenia (the economy from the group to see the smallest increase in GDP per capita but nonetheless remain above the world average) to 72.3% for Latvia (the most successful economy). All 10 are transition countries that managed significantly to reduce their backwardness, measured in the ratio of the change in their GDP per capita against the change in that of the EU-15.

These transition countries/new EU members' Chinn-Ito index scores show that the following countries have carried out full de jure liberalization of their current account and capital account transactions: Estonia (1998–2014), Latvia (2003–2014), the Czech Republic (2002–2014), Hungary (2005–2014), Bulgaria (2007–2014), and Romania (2007–2014).[12] Between 1997 and 2007, Lithuania applied full de jure financial openness, but reintroduced partial restrictions during the crisis (Ka_open for 2012–2014 of 69.70). The Slovak Republic has also retained partial controls (Ka_open for 2007–2014 of 75.28).

The cases of two fairly characteristic transition countries that became EU members in 2004 are particularly interesting from the perspective of de jure financial openness. Measured by GDP per capita, Slovenia is the most advanced transition country and was the first former socialist country to meet all the conditions to become a Eurozone member (January 2007). Its normalized Ka_open score for 1997 to 1999 was 41.11 (a de jure relatively financially closed economy), while from 2000 to 2002 it increased the degree of de jure financial openness (a normalized Ka_open of 69.70), so that by the year of reception into the Eurozone (2007) it was fully in compliance with de jure financial openness requirements. That year the normalized Ka_open index was 100. In the recession year (2009) Slovenia reintroduced partial controls over capital flows due to growing problems with external debt and contaminated assets in the banking sector, its three largest banks being in predominantly the government ownership. Since the banking sector crisis had a direct impact on Slovenia's public debt crisis, the country introduced additional legal restrictions on capital flows during both 2012 and 2013 (the normalized Ka_open for both years was 69.7).

Poland is the only EU transition country not to have gone into recession in 2009. It is also the most populous transition country to be a member of the EU (and has the largest population in Central and South-eastern Europe). Between 1996 and 2001, Poland was de jure a fairly financially repressed economy (its normalized Ka_open was 16.38). Over the following thirteen years to 2014, it retained significant legal control over international capital flows (the normalized Ka_open was 44.9). With regard to de facto financial openness, as measured by TOTAL, however, Poland increased the ratio of the sum of assets and liabilities registered in its International Investment Position to GDP from 84.3% in 2000 to 102.5% in 2005, 143.1% in 2010, and 155.5% in 2014. Total assets plus liabilities in 2000 were US$144.8 billion. By 2010, this had risen by US$541 billion, while over the next four years, it rose by an additional US$129 billion. Total liabilities and total assets were thus up 496% and 389%, respectively. In 2000, total liabilities were US$55.2 billion more than total assets, but by the end of 2014 the gap had increased to US$376.5. So, Poland's negative NIIP increased 583% between 2000 and 2014. FDI and loans (both short and long term) dominate the structure of liabilities. The cumulative value of inward FDI rose from US$34.2 billion in 2000 to US$255.7 billion in 2014 (647%). In other words, its NIIP to GDP ratio was (−19.9%) in 2000 and (−48.8%) fourteeen years later.[13]

When the countries of Central, Eastern, and South-eastern Europe began their transition from planned to market economies from the beginning of the 1990s through the first half of 2000s, the packages of measures included liberalization of the laws on FDI and the privatization of enterprises and banks (as well as trade liberalization, which was also conducted in most of these countries). The measures to liberalize trade and financial flows also entailed relatively rapid privatization of the banking sector. Liberalizing long and short-term capital flows and banking sector privatization in the countries that became EU members between 2004 and 2013 led to rapid growth in FDI, particularly in the countries of Central Europe and the Baltic. Rising FDI in these countries was based on the dominant role of FDI in the service sector, particularly banking. One consequence has been that banks dominate the financial sector in the EU13, whose banking sectors are in turn largely owned by banks from Western Europe (Italy, Austria, Germany, France).

There was, as a result, a direct transfer of knowledge and technology from the banking industry in Western Europe to the countries of Central, Eastern and South-eastern Europe, through Western banks' subsidiaries and sub-offices in the region. In this way, the sharp rise in lending in Western Europe lead directly to a relative abundance of additional liquidity in Central and Eastern Europe, with the extension of credit lines from parent banks to subsidiaries and a consequent sudden expansion in lending there. One result was a sharp increase in de facto financial openness. As most of the new EU members from 2004, 2007, and 2013 had fully or largely de jure liberalized their financial markets in preparation (excluding Poland and Slovenia), the consequent intensive growth of FDI into the financial sector (and other services) opened up access to capital in these countries. Their economic growth was largely based on domestic demand-led growth, supported by the rapid expansion of lending between 2002 and 2008 and a consequent growth in (most of) their current account deficits. By 2014, all of the EU-13 were de facto financially open. In terms of their TOTAL scores, the country with the highest gross capital flows to GDP ratio was Hungary. Its score was 579%, comparable to Denmark's score (556%) for the same year (2014).[14]

The fastest-growing economy in transition and the 20th fastest-growing country in the world between 2000 and 2014, Latvia had already achieved a TOTAL score of 159% by the end of 2000. By the end of 2009, it was up by a factor of 1.76 to 284%, while by the end of 2014 it was at 299%. Estonia, the 39th fastest-growing economy in the world during that same period had a TOTAL score of 183% for the last year of the last century. It reached 304% by 2009 and 325% by the end of 2014. The EU 13 country with the lowest de facto financial openness was Romania (TOTAL score of 131% in 2014). On the other hand, their NIIP showed that all these countries were net importers of capital. The greatest importers of capital in the group, measured by the ratio of NIIP to GDP, were Croatia (–88.3%), followed by Hungary (–73.5%), Bulgaria (–72.3%), and Slovakia (–70%).

Turning to the EU-15 group, Sweden performed best between 2000 and 2014, measured in both relative and absolute changes to its economic status. While its Cg was down 0.45% in 2014 on 2000, this indicates that Swedish GDP per capita was growing at a rate just half a percentage point below the world average. Germany was the second most successful economy, growing at a rate of just 2.1% less that the world average, while the United Kingdom took third place, growing at 3.8% below the world average. Countries that saw a decline of more than 10% in their world economic standing, measured in change to the Cg, were France (10.9%), Luxembourg (11.3%), Spain (12.3%), Denmark (14.6%), Portugal (17%), Greece (18.5%), and Italy (23.4%).[15] Viewed against the background of the changes that took place after 2008/2009 (the great recession), the EU-15 countries that suffered a relative decline of more than 10% against the world average seem likely to face very significant structural problems in both the medium and longer term. Indeed, the Southern Euro-zone economies have already been facing such problems for seven years. Given that world GDP per capita growth was around 20.1% for 2000–2014, EU-15 countries that saw a decline of 17% or more in their Cg have not only fallen behind the world average, but have experienced an absolute decline in GDP per capita measured in constant 2005 US$. This includes Portugal, Greece and Italy.

Relative economic decline has been a characteristic of the Italian economy in all three sub-periods: 2000–2005, 2005–2009, and 2009–2014. The country experienced a relative economic decline of 5.1% during the first period, of 7.3% during the next four years, and 13.3% in the period from 2009 to 2014. By contrast, Greece saw relative economic growth of 9.7% (faster than the global average) in the first five years and continued to grow at a rate 1% above the world average over the next four, to experience a major economic fall only in 2009–2014. Its relative decline then amounted to 26.4%. Like Italy, Portugal experienced a relative economic decline in all three sub-periods, of 5.6%, 1.8% and 10.5%, respectively.

Given Ireland's special role in international capital flows as a "systemically important small open economy" with very high volumes of capital flows in both directions (the sum of total assets and liabilities), it is important to analyze the connections between the changes in its relative economic standing and the degree of de facto financial openness. During the final decade of the last century, Ireland was the sixth fastest-growing economy in the world. Its Cg at the end of 2014 was 5.8% down on 2000. In other words, during the fourteen years to 2014 it experienced rates of economic growth (measured in GDP per capita) much below the world average. Indeed, Ireland was just 134th in the world during those fourteen years. Its growth rates during the first five years of the century, however, were 7% faster than the world average. It was during the following four years that it experienced a relative decline of 9.6% and was among the ten worst performers in the world. Large-scale intervention measures, with a steep increase in public debt, IMF and EFSF loans and EU guarantees, reduced the rate of relative backsliding from 9.6% in 2005–2009 to 2.5% in 2009–2014. Thanks to this moderate rate of relative underperformance against the world average, Ireland was in fact the most successful EU-15 economy after Germany and Sweden in 2009–2014. Its Chinn-Ito index from 1980 to 1991 had been 41.11, but from 1993 it fully liberalized all current account and capital account transactions, pushing the index to 100.[16]

Germany was the only EU-15 economy to see *growth* in the Cg in 2014 against 2009 (of 3%), and the only economy, not just from the EU-15, but from the G-7 to achieve a rate of GDP per capita growth above the world average, as well as an employment rate higher in 2014 than before the recession. Germany also had the highest trade surplus. These economic trends have resulted in a positive net investment position. In other words, Germany is one of the most important net lenders in the world. It has also traditionally been a leading advocate of free trade, as well as of free capital flows. Its normalized Ka_open has been 100 for the past forty-five years.[17]

During the first fourteen years of the current century, the EU-15 all did away with all restrictions on current account and capital account transactions. These economies were thus fully financially liberalized economies. De jure financial liberalization was accompanied by a steep increase in de facto financial openness. Excluding for the moment Cyprus, Ireland, Luxembourg, and Malta from consideration as specific financial hubs within the EU (and global financial flows), the average TOTAL score of the remaining EU-11 countries in the first year of the century was 307%. During the period of major credit expansion (the 2002–2008 period) capital flows between rich countries grew sharply both as increased borrowing and higher levels of FDI (principally focused on the service sector, with the lion's share going to the financial sector) and as portfolio flows. At the end of 2007, the average TOTAL measure for the EU-11 was up to 494% (see source of data below Table 5.1). The global financial shock in 2008 caused recession in these economies in 2009 (and in countries like Italy, Spain, Portugal and Greece in 2012–2013 as well). The battle against recession in most of the EU-11 (and EU-15) countries was based on expansionary fiscal and monetary policy.[18] Even if the institution's mandate from 2007 to 2014 for conducting an expansionary monetary policy was rather narrow compared with the Fed or the Bank of England, the measures taken by the ECB and by national and

Table 5.1 The TOTAL measure of financial openness for EU (Eurozone) countries: 2001–2014

Country	*2001*	*2007*	*2014*
Austria	296	562	539
Belgium	599	990	928
Finland	327	459	709
France	339	569	624
Germany	273	393	489
Greece	132	275	381
Ireland	1,388	2,492	4,145
Italy	183	262	300
Luxembourg	18,896	24,088	30,910
Netherlands	593	881	2,160
Portugal	308	456	498
Slovenia	105	233	257
Spain	221	356	374
Cyprus	445	763	1,217
Malta	459	1,068	5,488

Source: The author's calculations based on Eurostat data on the assets and liabilities of EU countries and GDP for the year 2014; the author's calculations based on data for the years 2001 and 2007 published in International Monetary Fund (2008). Data for GDP for 2001 and 2007 taken from the World Bank database available at: http://data.worldbank.org/indicator/NY.GDP.MKTP.CD

supra-national administrative bodies within the EU (EU country governments, the EFSF, the ESM), in cooperation with the IMF, produced an increase in financial flows back and forth between these countries, as well as between the EU countries and the rest of the world (including loans approved by the IMF to countries like Greece, Portugal, and Ireland). The result was an increase in the value of the average TOTAL score for the EU-11 from the aforementioned 494% in 2007 to 660% in 2014.

Table 5.1 gives the TOTAL measure for the 15 members of Eurozone for 2001, 2007 and 2014. Four of them, Cyprus, Ireland, Luxembourg, and Malta, had TOTAL scores significantly above the average of the remaining eleven in 2014. The difference in TOTAL score for Luxembourg and those eleven countries' average was particularly high. The volume of total capital flows through Luxembourg was almost 47 times the average for the 11 in 2014. The ratio of total capital flows to GDP was 6.3 times higher for Ireland than for those eleven countries on average for that year.

Percentage changes in TOTAL measure for 2001 to 2007, on the one hand, and 2007 to 2014, on the other, show that the country with the fastest growth in this indicator in the latter period was the Netherlands.[19] While total capital flows for this country grew by 49% against GDP in the first seven years of the century, the increase over the next seven years was 145%. This major growth in total capital flows was not accompanied by an improvement in relative economic standing between 2009 and 2014. Table 5.2 shows that the Netherlands, Greece, Cyprus and Finland were the worst performers in terms of how efficiently these capital flows were being used for counter-cyclical economic policy. The Netherlands and Finland

Table 5.2 Percentage change in the growth coefficients and total banking sectors assets of Eurozone countries (including foreign branches and subsidiaries): 2014/2009

Country	*Percentage change in the growth coefficient 2014/2009*	*Percentage change in total assets 2014/2009*
Belgium	-6.1	-16.3
Germany	+3.0	-18.2
Estonia	+13.1	-33.3
Ireland	-2.5	-62.4
Greece	-26.4	-24.7
Spain	-10.0	-4.2
France	-5.0	+13.8
Italy	-13.3	-0.4
Cyprus	-19.7	-47.2
Latvia	+13.5	+6.9
Lithuania	+18.8	-14.3
Luxembourg	-9.1	-8.5
Malta	-1.9	+20.9
Netherlands	-8.2	-4.5
Austria	-3.8	-5.4
Portugal	-10.5	-16.5
Slovenia	-7.9	-26.8
Slovakia	+4.4	+21.2
Finland	-7.3	+50.0

Source: Calculated by the author using ECB data from the ECB *Report on Financial Structures*, October 2015, p. 60.

were also the only countries to see their TOTAL scores rise faster during the second period (2007–2014) than the first (2001–2007). Nonetheless, the Netherlands was the only EU-28 country with greater total assets than total liabilities in 2014, to the tune of 64% of GDP. In other words, from 2007 to 2014, the country was at all times a net exporter of capital. Its net investment position to GDP ratio was 75% greater than Germany's in 2014. On the other hand, the EU-28 countries with the largest imports of capital (the NIIP to GDP ratio) were: Cyprus (−165%), Greece (−122%), Portugal (−112%), and Ireland (−107%).

Table 5.2 shows changes in total banking sector assets in Eurozone countries, along with percentage changes in the growth coefficient, reflecting relative economic growth. On the basis of these data, the worst performer seems to have been Finland, which, in spite of enjoying the largest increase in banking sector assets in the EU-15 group (by 50%) over the last five years, nonetheless felt relatively behind the world average by 7.3%. The country with the greatest fall in total banking assets was Ireland. The decline in its total assets was 62.4%, which was a key reason why its public debt rose from approximately 23.9% to 127% of GDP between 2007 and 2013.[20] While Ireland has succeeded, over the past two years, in reducing its public debt to GDP ratio to 93.8%, the "social cost" imposed on taxpayers there because of corrupt corporate governance in some of the leading banking groups in the country has been very great indeed. After Ireland, the Eurozone countries with the fastest-growing public debt to GDP ratios in 2007–2013 were (the numbers in the brackets indicate the factor by which the ratio increased over the six years in question): Latvia (4.7), Slovenia (3.1), Luxembourg (3), Lithuania (3), and Spain (2.6).

The highest degree of positive correlation between relative economic decline and decline in banking sector assets was to be found in Greece, Cyprus, Austria, and the Netherlands. On the other hand, Estonia was the most successful country, insofar as, in spite of a major fall (one third) in banking sector assets, it grew 13.1% faster than the world average. Because of its importance for the world economy, Germany also achieved exceptional results in this regard. The fall of 18% in its banking sector assets was accompanied not just by absolute, but by relative economic growth – at a rate 3% above the world average.

Notes

1. Source: The World Bank – available at: http://data.worldbank.org/indicator/NY.GDP.MKTP.CD
2. International Monetary Fund 2008; International Monetary Fund 2015.
3. Source: The author's calculations, based on World Bank data for the relevant years. Data available at: http://data.worldbank.org/indicator/NY.GDP.MKTP.CD
4. Data on assets and liabilities presented in the text for the two groups of countries are taken from the two IMF sources already cited in a previous footnote.
5. See IMF data in International Monetary Fund 2008, pp. 4–5.
6. Tarullo 2008, pp. 46–48.
7. See Gordon 1999.
8. See data on Nasdaq 100 available at: http://www.nasdaq.com/markets/nasdaq-composite
9. See: IMF 2000, Chapter III.
10. Source: The Federal Reserve Bank of St Louis – Economic Research: https://research.stlouisfed.org/fred2/series/IIPUSASSA (accessed on 10 May 2016).
11. Source: The Federal Reserve Bank of St Louis – available at: https://research.stlouisfed.org/fred2/series/IIPUSASSA
12. Nb. the time series for the Ka_open index ends with 2013.
13. All data on absolute values of total assets and total liabilities are taken from the National Bank of Poland's website on the International Investment Position available at: http://www.nbp.pl/homen.aspx?f=en/statystyka/m_poz_inwest.html
14. The author's calculation of TOTAL measure based on data published by the Eurostat and available at: http://ec.europa.eu/eurostat/statistics-explained/index.php/International_investment_position_statistics
15. The author's calculations based on the World Bank database.
16. See: http://web.pdx.edu/~ito/Chinn-Ito_website.htm
17. Source: http://web.pdx.edu/~ito/Chinn-Ito_website.htm (the value of Ka_open in column F multiplied by 100).
18. In this respect as well, Germany is an exception to the other countries in the group. Even if the German government did react in the recessionary year of 2009 by allowing the public debt to swell, it reduced it over the next five years, 2010–2014, by almost 5% of GDP.
19. Excluding Malta as a "special case", the biggest increase in TOTAL for 2007–2014 was in the Netherlands.

20. Source: Eurostat data on the public debt of Eurozone countries for the period are available at: http://ec.europa.eu/eurostat/tgm/table.do?tab=table&init=1&language=en&pcode=teina225&plugin=1

References

Gordon, R. J. (1999). Has the 'New Economy' rendered the productivity slowdown obsolete? Northwestern University and NBER. Revised Version (June).

International Monetary Fund. (2000, October). *World economic outlook*. Washington, DC: International Monetary Fund.

International Monetary Fund. (2008). International investment position: World and regional tables. Twenty-First Meeting of the IMF Committee on the Balance of Payments Statistics. Washington, DC (November 4–7).

International Monetary Fund. (2015, May 20). IMF Committee on balance of payments statistics 2014 annual report – Summary. Washington, DC: IMF.

Tarullo, D. K. (2008, August). *Banking on Basel – The future of international financial regulation* (pp. 46–48). Washington, DC: Peterson Institute for International Economics.

Websites

Eurostat: http://ec.europa.eu/eurostat/statistics-explained/index.php/International_investment_position_statistics http://ec.europa.eu/eurostat/tgm/table.do?tab=table&init=1&language=en&pcode=teina225&plugin=1

The Chinn-Ito Index: http://web.pdx.edu/~ito/Chinn-Ito_website.htm

The Federal Reserve Bank of St Louis: https://research.stlouisfed.org/fred2/series/IIPUSASSA

The National Bank of Poland: http://www.nbp.pl/homen.aspx?f=en/statystyka/m_poz_inwest.html

The World Bank: http://data.worldbank.org/indicator/NY.GDP.MKTP.CD

CHAPTER 6

Financial Liberalization and Globalization: Theory and Facts Over the Last Three Decades

It was forty-five years in August this year since the inconvertibility of the US$ into gold was declared. After the then US president, Richard Nixon, announced the decision, international financial markets reacted with a sharp decline in its value. This was a reaction to the "new world of international finances", which was to involve a considerably greater degree of uncertainty and unpredictability that the relatively stable and predictably international capital flows of 1945 to 1971, based on a dollar pegged to and convertible into gold. Once the US government had definitively announced in March 1973 that the currency was transferring to a free float exchange rate regime, the situation was no longer even remotely what it had been in the preceding twenty-eight years, the period immediately following the Second World War.

From the period of the Great Depression in the United States or more precisely from 1934, commercial bank deposit interest rates had been set in line with an official ceiling – in other words, the US government and Congress set the maximum interest rate US banks could pay depositors on domestic financial markets. The provisions of the law on "interest rate ceilings" ("Regulation Q") were only rescinded eleven years after the declaration of inconvertibility to gold (in 1982). The reaction on the financial markets to the decision finally to transfer to a system of floating exchange rates was to send the price of gold up sharply, with a concomitant fall in the value of the dollar, a sharp rise in the price of oil (the first oil shock) and accelerated inflation.

F. Čaušević, *A Study into Financial Globalization, Economic Growth and (In)Equality*, DOI 10.1007/978-3-319-51403-1_6

While, as shown in the preceding chapter, the United States was already fully open to international flows of goods, services and capital (the Ka_open for the United States has been 1 and its normalized value 100 since 1971), there was nonetheless partial financial repression on the domestic market – in other words, financial liberalization had not been completely implemented in the domestic banking sector. Economic theorists responded to the new situation in the world of international finance and on the domestic, partly repressed financial market in the United States by publishing a pair of early works on the topic of the impact of financial liberalization on economic growth. As we saw in Chapter 2, the terms financial repression and financial liberalization were introduced into economic theory by Ronald McKinnon[1] and Edward Shaw.[2] They published their works independently of each other precisely in the year in which the system of floating exchange rates was definitively established (1973). Their basic thesis was that financially repressed economies necessarily function at a sub-optimal level, given that the government-controlled interest rates on deposits limit savings. Lower savings mean less investment for the economy as a whole and less investment prevents long-term economic growth.

The basic conclusions of McKinnon and Shaw's academic works suggested that stimulating investment at the macroeconomic level by setting interest rate ceilings to increase the marginal efficiency of capital and of investment projects which are profitable only because the interest rates on deposits are depressed by law was unlikely to create a sound basis for the long-term sustainable growth of such investment projects. Financial liberalization and scrapping the laws that directly limit interest rates on deposits and loans thus become a key precondition for increasing savings and deposits in the banking sector, as a precondition to investment growth. Bank autonomy is another very important precondition of financial liberalization. According to this criterion, the entire banking sector should be privately owned, since private owners are better at managing their banks than the government, directing loans towards higher-yield projects which offer profits that are sustainable over the longer term.

As early as the 1950s and 1960s, before McKinnon's and Shaw's work had been published, Raymond Goldsmith[3] had written and published intensively on the topic of the impact of financial structures on economic growth in various countries around the world. In an article from 1959, he points out that financial structures must be taken into account in analysing the speed and direction of economic development.[4] The basic conclusions of his works from 1959 and 1969 were that financial structures are of major importance for economic growth and development, so that countries with "deeper" and more sophisticated financial systems have more options and a greater capacity for financing investment, allowing those economies in turn to take on more importance within international capital flows.

6.1 Financial Globalization and Developed Economies: Theory versus Facts

In the first chapter of their jointly edited book,[5] which presents an analysis of the interdependencies between the development of financial structures and economic growth, Demirguc-Kunt and Levine introduce their text by referring to these basic conclusions from Goldsmith's book from 1969. After a review of the topics dealt with in the book, the authors then draw a series of major conclusions. They point out that national financial systems become more complex and more developed as countries become richer. Their second conclusion is that the overall development of the financial system has a positive impact on economic growth, or rather that more-developed financial systems lead to accelerated economic growth, the formation of new firms, and easier access to financing. They stress the fact that data and research show that the efficiency of the legal system, its protection of investors, and the enforcement of contractual obligations are all of great importance for the development of financial systems. The third conclusion is that neither bank-based financial system nor market-based financial system (also called arm's-length) are *a priori* superior, so that neither of these two systems offers an in-principle better guarantee of faster economic growth.[6]

In analysing the links between a given financial system's degree of development and the rate of economic growth, it is particularly important to keep in mind their second and third conclusions, namely that the degree of development has a positive impact on economic growth, so that more-developed financial systems facilitate faster economic growth. This conclusion is particularly significant for the analysis presented in the preceding two chapters regarding the connections between economic growth and financial openness, as measured both by de jure and de facto measures. The results of our investigations into the relationships between financial openness and the rate of economic growth suggest that the following developed countries were amongst the 50 fastest-growing economies in 1990–2000 (their ranking by growth rate is given in brackets): Ireland (5th), South Korea (7th), Singapore (17th), Israel (18th), Norway (33rd), Portugal (44th), and the Netherlands (47th). The following developed economies were also growing faster than the world average: Spain (53rd), Hong Kong (56th), Denmark (57th), Austria (62nd), the United States (63rd), Australia (65th), the United Kingdom (67th), Cyprus (69th), Belgium (72nd), Finland (74th), Canada (76th), Sweden (78th), Greece (80th), France (83rd), Germany (85th), Iceland (86th), Italy (87th), and New Zealand (90th). Altogether, a total of 172 countries, for which data for the period in question was available, were ranked.[7]

The financial systems of the five developed countries among the 50 fastest-growing economies (1990–2000) were predominantly bank-based. Of the 18 developed economies included amongst those from rank 50 to rank 90 and thus growing faster than the world average, the economies of the United States and the United Kingdom relied upon market-based financial systems, where capital and money markets played the main role in structuring the sources of financing for the real sector (as well as the costs of financing investment). A particular characteristic of that decade, however, was the positive correlation found in these 23 developed countries between the degree of financial liberalization, further deepening of financial markets (as against the level already attained), and the accelerated rate of economic growth. Consequently, one can confirm for that decade as Demirguc-Kunt and Levine's basic findings about the causality of development of the financial system and accelerated economic growth.

The results of our analysis of rates of economic growth during the fourteen years to 2014 are suggestive of very different conclusions regarding the connections between the development and complexity of financial systems and their impact on the speed of economic growth. Thus, between 2000 and 2014, the 50 fastest-growing economies included only three developed economies, one of which is not even an independent state: Macao (3rd), Latvia (20th), and South Korea (50th). The only developed economies in next 50 fastest growing (51–100) were Hong Kong (61st) and Singapore (64th). During those fourteen years, only four more developed economies achieved rates of economic growth higher than the world average: Slovenia (107th), Australia (109th), Iceland (110th), and Israel (112th). We may distinguish two subgroups among the remaining developed economies:

- Developed economies with economic growth below world average GDP per capita growth (i.e. relatively falling behind), and

- Developed economies with not merely negative relative rates of growth (a fall in the growth coefficient) but absolute declines (lower GDP per capita in 2014 than in 2000).

The following countries belonged to the first subgroup: Sweden (115th), Germany (121st), New Zealand (122nd), the United Kingdom (125th), Canada (129th), Austria (131st), the United States (133rd), Ireland (134th), Finland (136th), Japan (138th), Switzerland (139th), Malta (140th), Belgium (141st), Norway (142nd), the Netherlands (145th), France (148th), Luxembourg (149th), Spain (152nd), and Denmark (157th). The second subgroup includes: Portugal (164th), Cyprus (165th), Greece (169th), and Italy (176th). The total number of countries included in the ranking for the period from 2000 to 2014, based on available data, was 184.[8]

In a paper published in 2004, Kiyotaki and Moore presented three groups of economies distinguished by degree of financial deepening.[9] Their Θ-ϕ model relies upon a Θ coefficient, which signifies the amount of money investors in the real sector will be willing in future to allocate to pay off liabilities used to finance current investment projects. The coefficient is directly positively correlated to institutional stability and the efficiency of the legal regime (respect for contracts) and is expressed in a value from 0 to 1. A rise in the value of the coefficient means greater potential for economic growth. The ϕ coefficient is also limited to a range between zero and one. The greater the value of ϕ the greater the liquidity of the financial market, and so the lower the costs of converting illiquid into liquid financial instruments, which in turn implies a greater degree of financial deepening.

Kiyotaki and Moore distinguish between three phases of financial development depending upon the value of these two coefficients. The first type of economic system is cash-based, with a low level of trust in institutions of the system and in the enforcement of contracts, so that securities issues do not represent a common form of savings (ϕ is low). The second type is economies in which there is a high degree of trust in institutions and the legal order, so that the use of money market and capital market instruments, so-called red and blue papers, is both intensive and widespread. Actors in such economies are neither “liquidity constrained” nor “credit constrained”, but this does not necessarily mean that such economies have a higher level of output than those belonging to the next (third) level of financial development. Kiyotaki and Moore refer to this level as economies in which there is a high degree of trust in institutions and in the legal regime, but the cost of converting illiquid instruments into liquid ones is relatively high (ϕ is significantly less than unity), so that the degree of financial deepening is less than in the foregoing phase of the development of the economy and financial markets. The authors point out that economies in which both coefficients are close to unity and in which, consequently, the costs of converting illiquid to liquid financial assets are not particularly great, are not necessarily economies that are growing faster than those in which Θ is close to unity (institutionally stable economies with relatively stable legal regimes and high rates of economic growth), but where the cost of converting illiquid assets is high.[10]

This model is useful for understanding the problems that appeared between 2000 and 2008, when internationally active banks were sharply expanding their lending and transactions on derivative markets were expanding even more intensively. In the context of the Kiyotaki-Moore model, transactions on derivative markets (which the authors do not mention in their paper) should represent an additional channel or mechanism for increasing the facility of converting illiquid to liquid financial instruments. On the other hand, too high a value of Θ, which, as already pointed out, represents trust in the institutions of the system, would be one of the key reasons for a lack of adequate controls and supervision of financial markets and of the dominant actors on them, of the sort that brought such major "social cost" to all of the developed countries. The potential for misusing financial derivatives for regulatory arbitrage offered by an environment of completely liberalized financial flows contributed to the steep expansion in speculative activities, used much less in the developed economies to finance investment projects, increase average productivity and promote sustainable growth than to insure the major internationally active financial groups against risk and increase their profits. Comparison of the volumes of developed and developing countries' financial flows in both directions (assets and liabilities in the international investment position) has shown that almost all the developed countries saw their IIP to GDP ratio increase sharply, with falling or negative growth rates, during the last ten, but more particularly the last five years (except for Germany).

To illustrate more clearly the changes in economic power and the financial resources which finance economic growth, the following three graphs show measurements for relative changes in the economic status of the G-10 countries over three sub-periods: 2000–2005, 2005–2009,

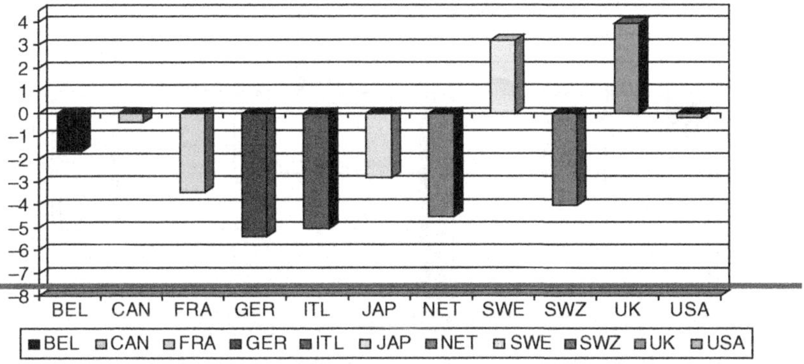

Fig. 6.1 Relative economic performance of the G-10 countries: 2000–2005 percentage change in the value of the growth coefficient for the G-10 countries and the threshold percentage change in the value of Cg distinguishing between relative and absolute economic decline

Source: Prepared by the author based on World Bank data.

and 2009–2014. These measurements are percentage changes in the growth coefficient for this group of countries, with the horizontal line on each of the three graphs representing the percentage fall in the Cg which marks the "threshold" between those countries experiencing a fall that signifies relative economic decline, as GDP per capita was growing more slowly than the world average, but still growing, and those countries which experienced not just a relative, but an absolute decline. Thus, the countries "below the red line" experienced an actual decline in GDP per capita as measured in constant US$ from 2005 and current prices.

During the first five years of this century, all the G-10 countries experienced economic growth, with GDP per capita (measured in constant US$ 2005) greater in 2005 than in 2000. Figure 6.1 shows that only two were growing at a rate above the world average, however, as indicated by the positive values for the percentage change in their Cg. The greatest "winner" in the group during these first five years was the United Kingdom, followed by Sweden. The other nine were growing at a rate slower than the world average. The declines in the Cg for the United States and Canada were 0.18% and 0.41%, respectively. In other words, their GDP per capita growth was just a bit lower than average

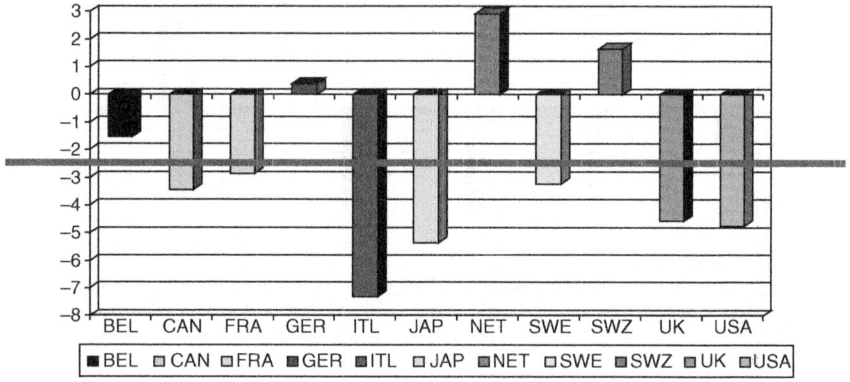

Fig. 6.2 Relative economic performance of the G-10 countries: 2005–2009 percentage change in the value of the growth coefficient for the G-10 countries and the threshold percentage change in the value of Cg distinguishing between relative and absolute economic decline

Source: The author's construction based on World Bank data.

world growth. On the other hand, the G-10 countries with greater relative declines and so falling behind world GDP per capita more significantly during this period included Germany, Italy, and the Netherlands. As we have noted, the horizontal line at the value of (−7.58%) marks the threshold value at which relative decline translates into absolute decline. As the figure shows, during the first five-year period none of these countries experienced the lag behind the world average required to put them in recession, i.e. a lower value of GDP per capita in 2005 than in 2000.

In contrast to these first five years, both the relative and absolute economic standing of the G-10 countries changed significantly over the next four. The threshold value of (−2.4%) for this period marks the difference between countries with a merely relative decline and those which have fallen behind in absolute terms. Figure 6.2 shows that only three members of the group attained rates of GDP per capita growth above the world average (which during this period was 2.58%): the Netherlands, Switzerland, and Germany. The only country in the group to see a reduction in the Cg that was nonetheless still less than the "the threshold decline" was Belgium (a fall of 1.58%). The other seven recorded declines of more than 2.4%, which meant their GDP per capita was lower in 2009 than it had been in 2005 (an absolute economic decline). The countries recording the greatest declines were Italy, Japan, the United States, and the United Kingdom.

Between 2009 and 2014, Germany and Japan were the only two countries from the group with GDP per capita growth faster than the world average rate. Germany's relative rate of economic growth was 3%, while Japan's Cg was up 0.18%. The marked expansionary monetary and fiscal policy pursued in the United States and the United Kingdom resulted in the absolute decline both countries faced in 2009 against 2005, which was however mitigated into a relative decline, with GDP per capita growth nonetheless lower than the world average. World average GDP per capita growth during this period was 8.2%.

Canada was also relatively successful in combating recession. In contrast to these countries, Italy and the Netherlands not only fell significantly behind in relative terms, but actually saw GDP per capita fall in 2014 compared to 2009 (Fig. 6.3).

To answer the question of how well the most-developed countries did in overcoming the crisis and in their counter-cyclical economic policies and what level of resources they spent to ensure GDP per capita was higher in 2014 than in 2009 and 2005 (the first year developing countries' foreign currency reserves outstripped those of developed countries), one

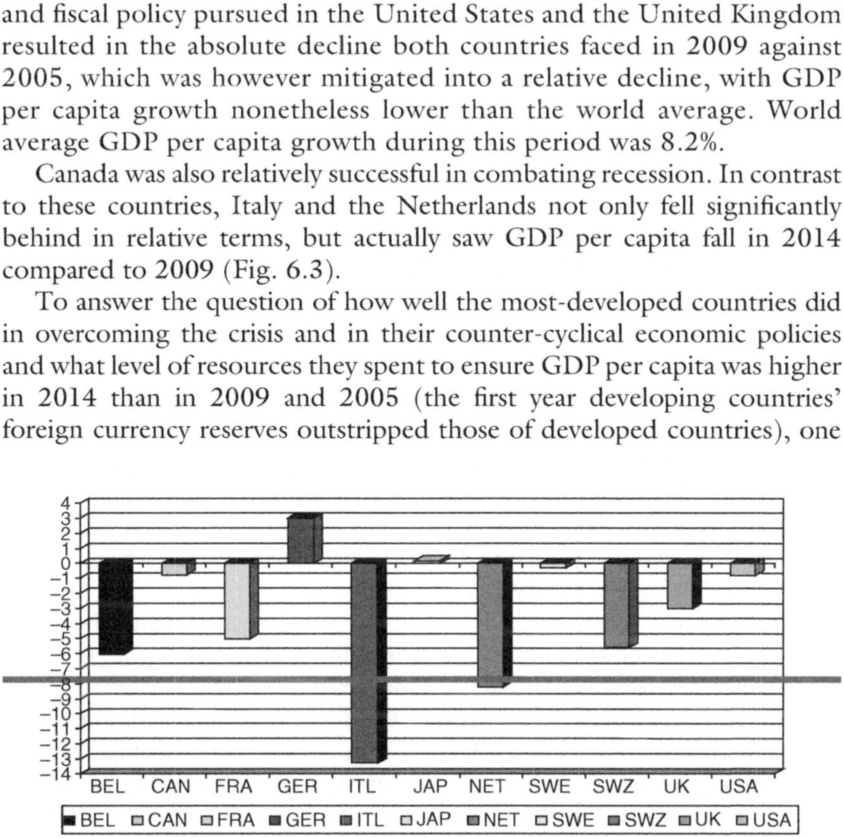

Fig. 6.3 Relative economic performance of the G-10 countries: 2009–2014 percentage change in the value of the growth coefficient for the G-10 countries and the threshold percentage change in the value of Cg distinguishing between relative and absolute economic decline

Source: The author's construction based on World Bank data.

must first compare their levels of public debt in 2005 with those accumulated nine years later (2014). The UK economy increased its level of public borrowing fastest and to the greatest degree. Its public debt to GDP ratio in 2014 was 112.5% higher than in 2005. Over the same period, the country's GDP per capita rose from \$39,935 (in 2005) to \$40,968 (2014), or just 2.6%. Consequently, every percentage increase in GDP per capita between 2005 and 2014 was accompanied by an increase in the level of the public debt of 43.3%. Looked at by sub-periods, 2005–2009 and 2009–2014, the level of public borrowing in the United Kingdom rose by 58.3% and 34.2%, respectively.

The G-10 economy with the next biggest increase in the level of public borrowing was the United States. The percentage increase in the value of its public debt to GDP ratio over the nine years in question (2005–2014) was 68.6%, while GDP per capita itself only went up from \$44,305 to \$46,405 or 4.7%.[11] Every percentage point increase in GDP per capita in the United States between 2005 and 2014 was thus accompanied by an increase in the level of the public debt of 14.6%. Between 2005 and 2009, the United States increased its public borrowing by 38.3%, while over the next five years it did so by 34.2%. Amongst EU G-10 members, it was France and the Netherlands which pushed up public borrowing most by 2014 on 2005 (by 42% and 39.5%, respectively). The most successful EU G-10 country in managing its public debt and the level of public borrowing was Sweden, whose public borrowing was in fact 7.1% lower in 2014 than it had been in 2005. The most successful country from the G-10 on this criterion was Switzerland, whose public debt fell 27.7% between 2005 and 2014.

After changes in the level of public debt and in measuring the effectiveness of the G-10 countries' economic policies and the financial resources used in their anti-recessionary drive, which necessarily have long-term consequences, we must now look at changes in the NIIP over the same period (2005–2014). With regard to percentage change in the NIIP to GDP ratio (net capital imports), the United States saw the greatest increase during these nine years, of 183%. More than 90% of this increase related to the period from 2009 to 2014. During the same period, the United Kingdom also saw a major increase in the negative value of its NIIP to GDP ratio: from (−8.7%) in 2005 to (−24.1%) in 2014. So, net import of capital to the United Kingdom against GDP was up 177%. In contrast to the United States and the United Kingdom, Germany's level of public borrowing rose a mere 11.7%, while GDP per capita was up 14.8%, and net export of capital (reflected in the positive value of the NIIP to GDP ratio) to the rest of the world was up 209.8%.

6.2 Financial Liberalization, Basel III and the New Capital Directive

The financial liberalization conducted by the United States in the 1980s (1980–1986), in combination with rapid development of the IT sector during the 1990s, laid the foundations for economic prosperity, turning a budget deficit into a budget surplus (1998 to 2001) and shrinking the public debt. As we have just seen, the United States improved its economic standing during the 1990s, at least compared to the 1980s. Given these results, the thesis of financial liberalization and globalization's positive impact on rapid growth, discussed by Demirguc-Kunt and Levine, appeared to have been and indeed was confirmed at least for the final decade of the last century.

At the end of his second presidential mandate Bill Clinton took two new key steps towards total liberalization of financial flows in the United States. The first was to do away with the only remaining "relic" in the American financial market system from Franklin Delano Roosevelt's time in government – the provision forbidding that investment banking be combined with the business of commercial banking. By signing the repeal of the Glass Steagall Act,[12] Clinton laid the groundwork for US financial groups to become universal financial services. The second key step towards complete liberalization of financial markets was a law he signed in December 2000, enabling a steep increase in transactions on derivative financial markets without the mediation of a central clearing house or central counterparty.[13]

The passage of these two acts (and the repeal of the Glass Steagall Act) has already been mentioned in Chapter 2. The enormous expansion in transactions on the OTC markets for financial derivatives during the first eight years of this century was a direct consequence of the law passed in December 2000 and, as became apparent during 2008–2009, it gave rise to major problems of non-transparency (and therefore risk) in contracting on this enormous market. Since there was no central counterparty for the clearing of positions, most of the transacting parties on the market had little or no real insight into whom they were agreeing transactions with. This is only part of the problem that came to the surface with the onset of the global financial crisis and the great recession. A chronic shortage in high quality collateral or high quality liquid assets caused problems in ensuring sufficient quantities of highly liquid financial assets when OTC-market contracts come due and it is time to clear positions. Since the major banking groups from Europe were also very active on US financial markets, it became a priority to deal with the problem of contaminated assets, in collaboration with the governments of the leading countries: the United States, EU countries, and Japan.

One response to the new situation was to adopt as a matter of urgency the new rules on capital adequacy for internationally active banks known as Basel III (2010),[14] along with the Dodd-Frank Act in the United States[15] and the Capital Requirement Directive IV (CRD IV)[16] in the EU. Since some of the largest and worst affected banks at the time of the global financial crisis in 2008 came from the EU (French, British, and German, especially the Deutsche Bank), the adoption of this series of new regulatory standards in response to the fundamental weaknesses of the Basel II rules and particularly those which had allowed internationally active banks to set their own capital to risk-weighted assets ratios on the basis of their own AIRB (Advanced Internal Ratings Based) and IRB (Internal Ratings Based) approaches (models) took place in rather a hurry. In addition to the LCR (Liquidity Coverage Ratio), Basel III significantly increased the requirements for regulatory capital and did away with the possibility allowed under Basel II that supplementary capital (Tier 2) equal core capital (Tier 1) in value. Under the Basel III rules, the role of Tier 2 is more strictly defined, with less room for manipulation than under Basel II.

A key contributory factor in the lead up to the global financial crisis was the very poor internal and external oversight of managerial structures in the main banking groups in both the United States and the EU (esp. in the period from 2002 to 2008, which was marked by major expansions in the property markets in the United States and parts of the EU, a simultaneous enormous expansion in transactions with financial derivatives, and a record high in lending by the major international banks). The fully adopted financial liberalization made possible in the United States by the laws Clinton signed in 1999 and 2000 and which was one of the fundamental priorities for EU and especially Eurozone member countries (under the Single European Act – Chapter I, the Second Banking Directive, and Maastricht Agreement – Article 56) helped create a problem of very weak internal controls in the major financial groups and went hand in hand with very poor external controls or oversight on the part of the national and supra-national regulators of financial markets.

Theoretical works by Jensen and Meckling (1976)[17] and Jensen and Ruback[18] have provided the basic explanation in the financial literature for the agency problem and agency costs, as well as for the motives behind and impact of the major expansion in merger and acquisition transactions. Roland Benabou and Jean Tirole[19] have also looked into the justification for the sharp increase in managerial remuneration and income levels for "talent" on the labour market, in the light of rising income inequality over the past three decades. Given that proof of the abuse of their market position by some of the most powerful private financial groups between 2009 and 2015 has not merely come to light, but has resulted in fines being imposed on banks amounting to hundreds of millions and even billions of dollars (in the United States) or euros or pounds (in Eurozone countries and the United Kingdom), it is clear that the ground for the problems that led to the global financial crisis, the great recession, and the sovereign debt crisis (in the EU) was prepared by the very weak system of internal controls between principal and agent, on the one hand, and superficial implementation of bank supervision (particularly in the area of asset quality review) and the great asymmetry in information available to regulators and the regulated, on the other.

One should, moreover, bear in mind that the "regulated" here are major financial groups and that they were so poorly supervised during the first decade of current century precisely because financial liberalization and the integration of financial services in all the more-developed economies created serious practical problems that made adequate supervision by the regulator de facto impossible, not least because the resources they had for recruiting "the best people" were inadequate compared to the financial resources at the disposal (then and now) of private banks for attracting "talent" and deploying it at least in part for purposes of regulatory arbitrage.

Given the goal of preventing management structures in the major financial groups from abusing their "agent" position to the disadvantage of "the principals", or, even worse, of entering into tacit coalitions with them, based on the calculation that the taxpayer will ultimately bear the costs of aggressive use of leverage to increase returns on equity through some form of bail-out precisely because of the financial group's importance (the too-big-to-fail market position), the directives passed by the European Council and the European Parliament represent one of the most important legal measures directed at preventing future abuses. Consequently, the BRRD[20] targets a key problem and one which was to a considerable degree fundamental in creating the greatest financial crisis since the Second World War.

It was the European Council and European Parliament's goal to use this directive to increase the responsibility for and quality of internal controls to a significantly higher level by obliging both shareholders and major creditors actively to require the management of financial groups to conduct business and structure financing more responsibly. Both these groups (shareholders and creditors) would be held responsible for making future losses – thus transforming a bail-out into a bail-in procedure. A look at the data of the Deutsche Bundesbank will illustrate how many direct and indirect interventions EU country governments have made and the costs incurred. In the report for 2014,[21] the bank states that EU members' total costs related to tackling the banking sector crisis amounted to EUR1.5 trillion (of which EUR591.9 billion was to recapitalize banks and other measures to consolidate banking sector assets, while EUR906 billion was given in guarantees). Even though the value of the guarantees issued has been reduced to EUR534.5 billion by 2012, the explicit and implicit costs imposed on taxpayers were clearly high.

6.3 Audacity of Hope: PFAS and Safe Assets

In chapter seven of his new book, the former governor of the Bank of England, Mervyn King[22] states that there is an urgent need for the international monetary system to be redesigned carefully in order to avoid financial shocks in the coming years. Discussing possible solutions to the problem of illiquidity at times of major financial shocks, he points out that the proposal for banking sector reform to prevent future crises put forward by the authors of the Chicago Plan Revisited,[23] which includes elements of a return to the golden rule of banking (a 100% reserve backing for deposits) and a separation of the monetary from the lending function in banking, fails to deal with the key problem facing the global financial system and the main banking groups in the leading economies today.

King's solution to the problems of the banking industry and the major (actual and potential) systemic risk arising from problems of the sharp decline in liquidity is that the leading central banks around the world should continue to develop unconventional monetary policy instruments and measures. More precisely, they should take on the role of "pawnbroker for all seasons" (PFAS) which would allow them to accept all asset items regardless of the degree of liquidity as collateral in approving new sources of liquidity, so not just liquid items. Under such circumstances, central banks would themselves set the discount rate (or haircut) for the various types or qualities of asset items lodged with them, thus significantly reducing one of the fundamental sources of insecurity on financial markets. Given that these institutions (the central banks) have the exclusive right under law to create money, which is to say new sources of liquidity, by expanding the categories of assets that they can accept as collateral, it will become possible to make sources of liquidity immediately available to actors within the system, while at the same time reducing the room for speculation ("the alchemy of finance").[24]

In the final section of his book discussed in Chapter I, Hyman Minsky offered his "Agenda for Reform", proposing a significantly more intensive use of discount-window operations than has been made to date of open market operations (even after the global crisis of 2008). His suggestion of thirty years ago is clearly not identical to King's, but was one of its "predecessors", as an idea directed at preserving financial stability by deploying types of bank asset that derive directly from business relations with the business sector as collateral for new loans by central banks. In line with this, King takes the view that the central bank function as classical lender-of-last-resort can no longer solve the problems of global (and major national) financial systems. There has been intense discussion since the turn of the century amongst financial experts within the IMF and in academic circles of a need to introduce an international lender of last resort. In an article from 2001, Adam Lerrick and Alan Meltzer proposed a transformation of the IMF into an international quasi-lender of last resort. Their key proposal was that the IMF would not actually have to turn itself into a classical lender of last resort, but the goal was the creation of temporary guaranteed liquidity for the defaulted countries.[25] What they were proposing was therefore that all the governments of countries with balance of payment problems or problems paying off their debts should default and issue government bonds guaranteed by the IMF instead. The securities would remain liquid and their price would rise (because of the IMF guarantee), while creditors would be compensated through ownership of financial assets of a higher quality and a significantly lower level of risk, again given the IMF guarantee. The institutional reputation of the IMF would of course be a key as "backing" for the government bonds of the defaulting countries.

At the time Lerrick and Meltzer were making their proposal, there were no crises on the horizon of the dimensions of the global financial crisis of 2008 or the sovereign debt crisis in the EU of 2010 to 2012. During those crises, the IMF did not in fact function as quasi-lender of last resort (as per the Lerrick-Meltzer proposal), but it did react relatively rapidly to the crisis, steeply increasing the available resources for intervention in countries affected (including both developing countries and small open-developed economies). In an article from 2014 (there is a revised version from 2016), Ricardo Caballero and Emmanuel Farhi explain the shortage in "safe assets" as a key factor affecting lagging aggregate demand and (potentially) resulting in "long-run or secular stagnation". They demonstrate that under "zero lower bound" circumstances, with a reduced number of financial assets – that is of eligible financial assets that can be treated as safe assets, these assets' prices will grow, but the yields will fall to a very low level (or even become negative), creating a problem over the mid-term regarding the (in)consistency of monetary policy based on unconventional measures, on the one hand, and the central banks' ability and reputation to conduct effectively a policy of "forward guidance", on the other.[26] When central banks have to apply pre-announced changes in interest rates (forward guidance[27]), if sufficient amounts of safe assets are not available and growth in aggregate demand is consequently insufficient, central banks may be tempted not to apply the changes to interest rates they have already announced. This can adversely affect their credibility as the key determining factor in managing expectations on financial markets and have a major impact on the effectiveness of the monetary policy transmission mechanism.

The safety trap problem analysed by Caballero and Farhi can be mitigated or even solved by a suggestion put forward by King in his book. The experience with yields on Italian and Spanish government bonds issued during the period of acute sovereign debt crisis (in order to refinance maturing debt) and on the public debt of the countries of the Southern Eurozone more generally (the final quarter of 2011 and the first half of 2012) made clear the importance of supra-national institutions' institutional capacity and, more particularly, of extending the authorities of the ECB. Under the then current regulations, this institution was prevented to purchase government securities from Eurozone member countries, but, because of sharply rising required returns on Italian and Spanish bonds at the end of 2011 (in a range from 5.8% to 6.2%), the ECB nonetheless intervened by buying government bonds from Italy, Spain, Greece, Portugal and Ireland on secondary capital markets. These purchases stimulated demand and caused the price of the bonds to rise, bringing down the cost of refinancing their public debt.

During the second half of January 2015 (22 January), the ECB was given a clear right to purchase the government bonds of all Eurozone countries as well as of eligible companies from the real sector (2016), which has brought about radical change in the composition of this institution's balance sheet over the last two years, in favour of a sharp rise in the role of government bonds, as a consequence of the QE1 programme (begun March 2015), extended in November 2015 to the end of March 2017 (originally it was to end in September 2016). The European Stability Mechanism (ESM) is a supra-national institution established by the EU for the purposes of financial intervention in Eurozone countries affected by the crisis. This institution, which inherited the roles of the EFSF and the EFSM, along with a total capital of EUR700 billion, EUR500 billion of which is available for financial intervention in Eurozone countries affected by the crisis, is thus also a supra-national institution whose fundamental task is to bypass capital markets when Eurozone countries (and their banks) find their access to those markets significantly hindered because of falling confidence in those countries' institutions and, consequently, falling prices for and rising yields on government bonds and a consequent rise in budgetary expenditures.

The ESM is a typical example of the supra-national institutions that have sprung up during the period of the sovereign debt crisis in the EU. It enjoys a high degree of trust on the part of investors in money and capital markets and the highest possible rating for any issue of its own bills, notes or bonds. By issuing its own short-maturity bonds (between 6 and 30 months), the ESM raises financial resources which it then places at a considerably longer maturity term with crisis-affected countries. For the purposes of illustration, we may cite the financial aid package extended to Spain to help recapitalize the country's banking sector. The financial package approved by the ESM for Spain to recapitalize the banking sector amounted to EUR100 billion. Spain used EUR41.3 billion of this package. The way the ESM secured the resources was by issuing bills (with maturities of 2 and 10 months) and floating rate notes (with maturities of between 18 and 36 months).[28] The repayment term for the loans extended to Spain on the basis of the resources collected in this way by the ESM was 12.5 years. In this way, a fall in prices and an increase in yields on Spanish government securities, whose institutional stability was assessed by financial investors as considerably lower than it had been in the pre-crisis period, could be bypassed thanks to the institutional reputation of the ESM and its Triple-A status, which it received as a supra-national institution of the EU and which allowed it to access resources at significantly lower cost and so help Spain manage the crisis in its banking sector considerably more easily.

The ESM is also a good example of a new form of supra-national institution whose reputation on the markets is high and which can, consequently, increase the number and type of "safe assets" issued to capital markets. So, given that the securities issued by the ESM are issued by an institution that has received the highest possible (Triple-A) rating from the Basel Committee for Banking Supervision, any such issue represents an increase in the supply of safe assets. Even if issues of securities by this and other supra-national financial institutions are less common than issues of government bonds in either developed and developing countries, the very existence of such institutions promotes an increase in the supply of secure or less risky financial assets. A fall in the rating of government securities in developed countries (during the period of sovereign debt crisis in the EU, the typical examples were from southern Eurozone countries) also means a significant contraction of available financial assets acceptable to the Basel Committee for Banking Supervision as high-quality liquid assets. Consequently, increasing the supply of securities issued by supra-national financial institutions with the highest rating (thanks to their institutional stability because of the broad circle of founding countries and their initial capital) represents at least partial compensation for the dip in the supply of safe assets by the governments of developed countries affected by the crisis. Precisely for these reasons any future development of the global financial system should be based on a network of guarantee schemes and guarantee funds established by the most stable economies in the world, on the one hand, and supra-national institutions or groups of countries, on the other hand, which would then be able to guarantee future issues of government securities or bonds by small open developing economies or developing economies more generally which do not happen to belong to any supra-national integration (like the EU).

6.4 A Proposal for the Issuance of Safe Assets in Developing Economies

Most developing economies, but particularly small open developing economies which are not members of the European Union or of any particular significance in international capital flows, face more or less acute problems of insufficient institutional stability or indeed continuous instability, accompanied by frequent changes in government and consequently inconsistent government programmes. It is also often required of such countries that they implement market reforms, like the liberalization of their financial systems or developing corresponding institutions, and so increase their attractiveness to FDI, within very short time frames. We have already seen that the group of small open economies that enjoyed rapid growth during the fourteen years to 2014 did not achieve that rapid growth exclusively on the basis of liberalizing their trade and financial flows. Liberalization was an important aspect of these countries' economic policies, but the strategic position and strategic interests of the most populous developing countries, on the one hand, and of investors from the West, on the other, were very significant factors in "taking their positions" for the years to follow. Countries in transition (the former socialist countries) offer good examples of the positive correlation between rapid financial opening-up and accelerated economic growth, but equally of how the model of rapid growth based upon credit expansion, as a result of financial liberalization and connections with Western European banks, combined with de-industrialization and increasing FDI into the service sector to stimulate domestic demand-led growth, has created a problem of maintaining external liquidity, because of the rapid growth of the current account deficit.

The reform package on which the international financial institutions have insisted for developing countries, whether in Europe or in other continents, entails increasing transparency in public spending, the development of financial market institutions, which should be focused on stimulating faster rates of economic growth, and on reducing the differences in the distribution of wealth. Rapid liberalization of trade and financial markets were the "standard demands" of the major global financial institutions. These packages were not, however, accepted by the more populous developing countries. The development of financial markets as an integral part of the macroeconomic policies of developing countries and more particularly of small open developing countries has and continues to run up against problems of insufficient supply of safe or relatively safe financial assets to provide a basis for the efficient portfolio management of financial investors (investment funds, pension funds, insurance companies, investment banks). One consequence of this is a flight of capital into developed countries "in search of" safe or safer forms of financial asset. A solution to this flight of capital and the consequent lag in economic growth might be for the European Union and other developed countries (the United States, Japan), in cooperation with the international financial institutions, to set up guarantee funds for developing countries and particularly for small open developing economies, whether in Europe (for example the countries of the Western Balkans), or in the countries of Central and Southern Asia, Africa, or South America. This proposal is based upon an article the author of this book published in 2012 regarding the countries of the Western Balkans.[29]

Safe assets for small open developing economies are based on the idea of establishing guarantee funds (an EU Guarantee Fund for the Western Balkans in case of the Western Balkans) which would guarantee the issuance of government bonds by developing countries in exchange for a threefold possibility of controlling public finances and the use of financial resources. First, such guarantee funds would have a right to guarantee/equity swaps, so that these funds would be able to convert the liabilities under guarantee, once activated, into equity in public companies in majority state ownership with secure cash flow or companies managing natural resources in developing countries. In Western Balkan countries those would be companies from the power generation and distribution sector or telecommunications, while in Central Asian countries and in some African countries they might be state-owned companies for oil and gas exploitation or companies with a right of management over natural resources like forests or water. So, the first instrument of effective control guarantee funds established by such partners as the EU, United States, Japan, China, IBRD, EBRD, etc., would have at their disposal would be their right to guarantee/equity swaps.

The second effective instrument of control at their disposal would be possession of golden shares in all public companies whose assets had been pledged against government securities issued by developing countries. These government bonds would be denominated in the national currency. The third instrument they would have in all regions of the world where they might be established would be a direct right of control over the use of public funds and in particular the allocative use of the financial resources raised by issuing bonds with such a guarantee. Such bond issues would be used exclusively to finance capital projects (their maturity would be at terms of ten, twenty or thirty years), which would entail financing infrastructural development, as well as the development of business clusters, and including financing for research and development. Since the most stable countries or groups of countries in the world (e.g. the EU) and the most important international financial institutions (the World Bank, the IMF) would be standing guarantee for these bond issues, they could, under international banking rules (Basel III), be given a high rating (double or triple A). Thanks to this status, these bonds would command a good price and the yields required would be considerably less than for any bonds they might have issued in the past without effective supervision by major world financial institutions or countries/groups of countries.

This would make the use and distribution of public funds easier to monitor, whether by direct monitoring of the use of resources raised through issuing the bonds or by improving the quality of corporate procedures and governance in public companies thanks to holding the golden share. At the same time, it would eliminate the pressure on developing countries to privatize all their assets and natural resources in the short to medium term, particularly assets in sectors that are profitable and enjoy positive cash flows, since experience in recent decades suggests that the preference for privatization on the grounds that private owners (shareholders) necessarily run companies better has no firm basis, at least in most transition or developing countries. If the governments of developing countries issuing such guaranteed bonds perform poorly during periods of political turbulence and are consequently not able to refinance liabilities by issuing new bonds at equally favourable interest rates, the guarantee funds could "collect" on debt payments these governments cannot regularly service by activating the conversion of their guarantees into equity, taking over majority control and managing the public companies and their financial results. In this case, the point is that the founders of the guarantee funds would be able to collect on liabilities relatively easily, while at the same time helping any countries for whom they had issued such guarantees to weather crises and realize common interests on a partnership basis. In this way, the growing supply of "safe assets" in a series of developing countries would allow both local and international financial investors access to a significantly broader selection of safe assets and therefore to structure their portfolios more successfully, while at the same time facilitating the financing of economic development on more favourable terms on domestic financial markets in developing countries, while reducing the demand for government bonds of the more-developed countries, which creates problems of rising prices and very low yields (or negative yields).

Notes

1. McKinnon 1973.
2. Shaw 1973.
3. Goldsmith 1969.
4. Goldsmith 1959, pp. 114–123.
5. Demirguc-Kunt and Levine 2001, Chapter I, pp. 1–12.
6. Demirguc-Kunt and Levine 2001, pp. 11–12.
7. The author's calculations based on the World Bank database.
8. The author's calculation based on the World Bank database.
9. Kiyotaki and Moore 2005, pp. 701–713.
10. Kiyotaki and Moore 2005, p. 703.
11. Note: GDP per capita is measured in current prices and constant US$ from 2005.
12. By signing the Gramm-Leach-Bliley Act (the Financial Services Modernization Act /12 November 1999) then US president Bill Clinton repealed the Glass-Steagall Act from 1933 and allowed financial groupings in the United States to unite all forms of financial mediation under a single roof.
13. The Commodity Futures Modernisation Act was also signed by Bill Clinton (21 December 2000) a month before formally handing over the reins of government to his successor George W. Bush.
14. See: Basel Committee on Banking Supervision 2010, revised version June 2011, available at: http://www.bis.org/publ/bcbs189.pdf
15. The full text of the Dodd-Frank Wall Street Reform and Consumer Protection Act is available at: https://www.sec.gov/about/laws/wallstreetreform-cpa.pdf (dated 5 January 2010).
16. The Capital Requirement Directive IV was published in the Official Journal of the European Union on 23 June 2013. Available at: http://eur-lex.europa.eu/legal-content/EN/TXT/PDF/?uri=CELEX:32013L0036&from=EN
17. Jensen and Meckling 1976. E-version available at: http://papers.ssrn.com/sol3/papers.cfm?abstract_id=94043
18. Jensen and Ruback 1990.
19. Benabou and Tirole 2013.
20. The European Parliament 2014, available at: http://eur-lex.europa.eu/legal-content/EN/TXT/PDF/?uri=CELEX:32014L0059&from=EN
21. Deutsche Bundesbank 2014, p. 93.

22. King 2016.
23. Kumhof and Benes 2012.
24. King 2016, pp. 269–281.
25. Lerrick and Meltzer 2001, available at: http://repository.cmu.edu/cgi/viewcontent.cgi?article=1032&context=tepper
26. Caballero and Farhi 2014. A new version from May 2016 is available at: http://www.nber.org/papers/w19927.pdf
27. On forward guidance and efficient communication strategies for central banks see Woodford 2013, available at: http://www.columbia.edu/~mw2230/RiksbankIT.pdf; Woodford 2005.
28. See the financial arrangement on the ESM website: http://www.esm.europa.eu/assistance/spain/
29. Čaušević 2012.

References

Basel Committee on Banking Supervision. (2010, December). *Basel III: A global regulatory framework for more resilient banks and banking systems.* Bank for International Settlements. A revised version June 2011.

Benabou, R., & Tirole J. (2013, April). *Bonus culture: Competitive pay, screening, and multitasking* (Working Paper 18936). National Bureau of Economic Research.

Caballero, R. J., & Emmanuel F. (2014, February). *The safety trap* (Working Paper 19927). Cambridge, MA: National Bureau of Economic Research.

Čaušević, F. (2012). What type of fiscal policy for the Western Balkans during the crisis? *Southeast European and Black Sea Studies, 12*(2), Routledge, Taylor&Francis Group, 357–372.

Demirguc-Kunt, A., & Levine R. (Eds.). (2001). Financial structure and economic growth: Perspectives and lessons. In *Financial structures and economic growth: A cross-country comparison of banks, markets and development* (pp. 1–12). MIT Press. Chapter I.

Deutsche Bundesbank. (2014, November). *Financial stability review 2014.* Germany: Frankfurt am Main.

Goldsmith, R. W. (1959). Financial structure and development as a subject for international comparative study. In National Bureau of Economic Research (Ed.), *The comparative study of economic growth and structure* (pp. 114–123). Washington DC: NBER.

Goldsmith, R. W. (1969). *Financial structure and development.* London: Yale University Press.

Jensen, M. C., & Meckling, W. H. (1976). Theory of the firm: Managerial behavior, agency costs, and ownership structure. *Journal of Financial Economics, 3*(4), 305–360.

Jensen, M. C., & Ruback, R. S. (1990). The market for corporate control: The scientific evidence. In C. W. Smith (Ed.), *The Modern Theory of Corporate Finance* (pp. 593–638). McGraw-Hill.

King, M. (2016). *The end of alchemy – money, banking, and the future of the global economy.* London: Little Brown.

Kiyotaki, N., & Moore, J. (2005, April-May). Financial deepening. *Journal of the European Economic Association, 3*(2–3), 701–713.

Kumhof, M., & Benes, J. (2012). *The Chicago plan revisited* (IMF Working Paper No.12/202). Washington, DC: The International Monetary Fund.

Lerrick, A., & Meltzer, A. H. (2001, October 22). *Blueprint for an international lender of last resort.* Tepper School of Business, Carnegie Mellon University.

McKinnon, R. I. (1973). *Money and capital in economic development.* Washington, DC: The Brookings Institution.

Shaw, E. S. (1973). *Financial deepening in economic development.* Oxford: Oxford University Press.

The European Parliament. (2014, June 12). The bank recovery and resolution directive. *Official Journal of the European Union.*

Woodford, M. (2005, December). *Central bank communication and policy effectiveness.* (Working Paper No. 11898). Washington, DC: National Bureau of Economic Research.

Woodford, M. (2013, May). Forward guidance by inflation-targeting central banks. Available at: http://www.columbia.edu/~mw2230/RiksbankIT.pdf

CHAPTER 7

Concluding Remarks: Financial Openness, Economic growth and (In)Equalities in the World

Our study of the interdependencies between financial openness and economic growth, on the one hand, and global (in)equalities over the past twenty five years, but particularly the first fourteen years of this century, on the other, has shown how shaky the initial assumptions made in early works on this topic in the 1970s, in particular the assumption of a positive correlation between development of the financial system, innovation and the rate of economic growth, became during the first fourteen years of the current century. More precisely, the research presented in this book demonstrates that while financial liberalization may have been a very important element of economic policy in the 20 fastest-growing countries during this period, most of them, and the two most populous ones, China and India, in particular, approached it only gradually. Certainly, neither China nor India could have achieved such exceptional results in growth rates, poverty reduction, and increasing their absolute and relative stakes in world economic flows without attracting significant amounts of export-oriented FDI. This is particularly true of China. But it is not less true that both countries did take a gradual approach to financial liberalization and the financial strength of their major banks (again particularly China) shows that gradually opening up to (minority) ownership of banks and banking institutions allowed them to introduce mechanisms to improve corporate practice, while also maintaining state control over the management of financial and economic cycles. Their policy raises the issue of the insufficient deepening and

F. Čaušević, *A Study into Financial Globalization, Economic Growth and (In)Equality*, DOI 10.1007/978-3-319-51403-1_7

sophistication of financial and, more particularly, capital markets at times when developing countries have become a major destination for international financial investors.

The results of our investigation into financial theory's fundamental assumptions regarding the impact of financial opening upon the practical aspects of managing financial stability, whether at national or global level, deserve attention, particularly with regard to the more financially sophisticated countries and generally speaking more-developed countries. The two financially most sophisticated environments – the United States and the United Kingdom – saw GDP per capita decline between 2005 and 2009, a fact that is not unconnected with the simultaneous major expansion in transactions on derivative markets and the major expansion of lending by internationally active banks. This directly contradicts the predictions of most papers published during the 1980s and 90s and even the first few years of this century.

A moderate relative decline, measured in percentage change in the growth coefficient, would not in itself be evidence of negative links between the degree of development of the financial system and the rate of economic growth. A relative decline accompanied by an absolute decline, however, does demonstrate that the problems which brought on the global financial crisis in 2008 and later the sovereign debt crisis in EU countries (and to a certain degree in the United States as well) have roots in fundamental aspects of the financial systems of the more-developed countries. The United Kingdom and the United States are the two countries most involved in transactions in financial derivatives from overall financial flows and, in contrast to Western Europe, their money and capital markets dominate the generation of real sector financing in them (arms-length financial systems). As a result, both the United States and the United Kingdom offered major opportunities for financial speculation based on the abuse of financial derivatives and regulatory arbitrage. Their recovery from the shocks in 2008 and 2009 required enormous financial packages, certainly in comparison to anything previously. Each individual percentage point of GDP per capita growth achieved between 2005 and 2014 was accompanied both by enormous growth in public debt and much more rapid growth in their negative net international financial positions (a steep increase in net foreign debt).

The preceding paragraph, with its brief statement of the fundamental paradox underlying the relationship between financial liberalization and economic growth in the two most financially sophisticated environments, does not mean financial liberalization in developed economies has to lead to economic stagnation and so lower or even negative growth rates over the longer-term. While it is a thankless task to project what relations between developed and developing countries will look like in the coming decade or two, it does appear from Germany's performance, particularly between 2005 and 2014, that completely (de jure) financially liberalized economies with high and growing levels of de facto financial openness (Germany's TOTAL is higher than the United States's) can avoid the problems of secular stagnation and economic backsliding.

Whatever indicator one looks at, from the rate of economic growth to reducing unemployment to the budget surplus, the data presented in this study show that fully de jure and de facto financially liberalized and open Germany performed best of all the developed countries. On the other hand, the second most important founder country in the EU – France – was not quite so successful. Social costs, measured by the rise in public borrowing to combat the great recession, were particularly high in France, resulting in a considerably weaker impact of financial openness and degree of globalization than in Germany. By contrast, the Netherlands offers an example of a country which had managed to improve its economic standing vis-à-vis the world average up to 2009 under conditions of full financial openness, which might lead one to conclude that the correlation between financial openness and economic growth in this country is positive. It had, however, not just experienced a relative decline by 2014, with a growth rate below the world average, but had actually seen GDP per capita fall against 2009. In spite of converting a negative net international investment position (2009) into a strikingly positive one (2014), the Netherlands thus nonetheless experienced a fall in GDP per capita.

The countries of the Southern Eurozone experienced strongly negative correlations between full financial liberalization and growth rates. It is one of the fundamental assumptions of financial liberalization that private sector banking always targets resources better, more efficiently and towards more productive uses than publicly-owned or mixed forms of banking. It is worth noting in this regard that the steep expansion in lending between 2002 and 2008 in Spain, Greece, Italy, and Portugal was based on incentives to invest in the commercial property sector associated with tourism and financial services. Over the medium term (1995–2005), this investment did contribute to rapid economic growth (during the period of abundant credit), but it also led to the development of major structural imbalances within the economies of the southern Eurozone and equally severe imbalances on their labour markets, which have resulted in absolute economic backsliding and an already lengthy recession, whose economic and political consequences over the next decades are far from certain.

In addressing the question of why Germany has been so successful, particularly over a period in which most other developed countries have been stagnating or have had to spend far more financial resources to bring about recovery, especially within the EU context, one finds at least part of the answer in the structure of their financial systems and real sectors, including the composition of FDI into them. Over the past five years, the five largest banks in Germany accounted for approximately 25–30% of the banking sector. By contrast, banking sector concentration in France was such that the five largest banks accounted for more than 50%, while in Spain it was more than 60% and in the Netherlands more than 80%. Even if the number of lending institutions in Germany has gone down over the past five years from 1900 to approximately 1700 (according to data published by the ECB), it is still four times greater than in France and three times greater than in Italy, even though Germany's population is only 23% more than France's and 33% more than Italy's.

As to FDI, investment in export-oriented manufacturing between 2000 and 2011 was twice as high in Germany as in the United Kingdom. Consequently, we find ourselves unable to confirm for the first fifteen years of the current century the answer given in the final two decades of the past century to one of the major research questions posed in academic works from the 1960s and 70s regarding the importance of financial structures and their impact on economic growth. The answer then was negative, i.e. that in and of themselves financial structures neither contribute to the acceleration of growth nor cause slower growth. We can no longer claim this, as financial structures in which financial innovation dominates (because of the major role of financial derivatives) and which have seen considerable deepening of arm's-length markets or banking systems with high degrees of concentration within five major banks (resulting in an inflexible financial system) have given rise to significantly higher social costs related to combating recession, as represented by the major growth in public debt and/or net foreign borrowing and significantly lower or even negative growth rates, than financial systems with a far lower degree of market concentration in the banking sector (Germany).

The 20 fastest-growing economies during the first fourteen years of the century were mostly developing or poor countries (18 of 20). Their financial systems and the degree of financial liberalization and financial openness differed considerably. Most of them, however, achieved rapid economic growth by attracting capital from abroad through FDI. For some, FDI growth was linked to a sharp increase in foreign borrowing, while a number of small open fast-growing countries managed to reduce their foreign debt. This is particularly true of oil and gas producing countries, whose rapid economic growth was largely based on a combination of more intensive exploitation of energy resources and rising prices for them (up until 2013), as well as an increase in FDI in those sectors. As regards de facto measures of financial openness, most of these countries saw a major increase in overall capital flows as a proportion of GDP. With regard to de jure measures of financial liberalization, however, most developing countries were more or less financially repressed, with de jure financial opening-up primarily targeted at attracting FDI into manufacturing.

The two most populous countries in the world, China and India, placed consistently among the ten fastest-growing economies of the last twenty five years and China was one of the five fastest-growing economies for all five of the five-year sub-periods between 1990 and 2014. Both these economies approached financial liberalization gradually. As one of the fastest-growing economies and the first developing country to have its currency included into the basket of currencies used to calculate Special Drawing Rights (since December 2015, and effective from October 2016), China did not achieve higher growth rates *through* financial repression. Its economic success was due to targeted financial opening-up to investment in export-oriented manufacturing, with a coordinated attempt to integrate itself into international chains of production and added value. This was what allowed it to achieve such spectacular economic growth over the first ten years of this century. The significantly higher amounts of FDI over the past five years, compared to earlier periods, have been correlated with falling rates of growth, reflecting the fact that, during the higher phases of economic development, investment in the real sector requires more units of cash for each unit of output. This has happened just as loan-approval procedures in the megabanks, whose assets have grown even more rapidly than the rate of economic growth, are becoming less efficient, suggesting probable problems down the line with cleaning bank balance sheets.

Even though the 20 fastest-growing economies included 18 developing countries, data on changes in gross national income, measured in US$ purchasing power parity, suggests that the differences between countries generally, particularly the top 10% and the lowest 10%, have not in fact been reducing, but have continued increasing over the past twenty five years. The most striking reduction in differences between countries within a given continent over the first fourteen years of the century has taken place in Europe. Here the differences between the richest and poorest countries have practically halved. The differences in GDP per capita between countries within Asia, by contrast, increased during the final decade of the last century, to shrink during the first fourteen years of this one, but nonetheless remain practically twice those in Europe. The correlation between radically implemented financial liberalization and economic growth was most direct precisely in Europe and particularly Central and South-eastern Europe and the Baltic. The rapid implementation of financial liberalization, including full opening-up to FDI in the banking sector and privatization of that sector in these European regions led to a direct spill-over effect of the steep expansion in lending in the core countries (Western Europe) to easier credit by subsidiary banks in the peripheral regions (for the period from 2000 to 2008). The subsequent decline in lending also led to a decline in investment and economic stagnation in the post-crisis period in the regions except of the Baltic.

Appendix: Financial Globalization, Economic Growth and (In)Equalities

Table A. 1 Growth coefficients – world 1990 top down

Country	*Growth Coefficient (Cg) 1990*
1. Monaco	19.268
2. Liechtenstein	11.964
3. Bermuda	9.559
4. Luxembourg	8.812
5. Switzerland	8.652
6. United Arab Emirates	8.457
7. Norway	7.871
8. Iceland	7.176
9. Denmark	6.397
10. United States	5.711
11. Sweden	5.594
12. Japan	5.395
13. Netherlands	5.364
14. Andorra	5.185
15. San Marino	5.033
16. Austria	5.027
17. Finland	4.984
18. United Kingdom	4.981
19. Germany	4.979
20. Belgium	4.935
21. France	4.889
22. Canada	4.823

(*continued*)

F. Čaušević, *A Study into Financial Globalization, Economic Growth and (In)Equality*, DOI 10.1007/978-3-319-51403-1

Table A. 1 (continued)

Country	*Growth Coefficient (Cg) 1990*
23. Brunei Darussalam	4.642
24. Italy	4.582
25. Australia	4.333
26. Greenland	4.218
27. Ireland	4.115
28. Bahamas, The	3.879
29. New Zealand	3.638
30. Spain	3.314
31. Isle of Man	3.068
32. Hong Kong, SAR China	3.040
33. Singapore	2.865
34. Greece	2.737
35. Puerto Rico	2.561
36. Bahrain	2.526
37. Macao, SAR China	2.506
38. Portugal	2.465
39. Israel	2.336
40. Cyprus	2.293
41. Barbados	2.117
42. Saudi Arabia	2.112
43. Oman	1.813
44. Czech Republic	1.788
45. Antigua and Barbuda	1.672
46. Malta	1.671
47. Korea, Republic	1.528
48. Seychelles	1.520
49. Gabon	1.345
50. St. Kitts and Nevis	1.292
51. Mexico	1.129
52. Trinidad and Tobago	1.129
53. Russian Federation	0.984
54. Venezuela, RB	0.914
55. South Africa	0.877
56. Turkey	0.867
57. Poland	0.824
58. St. Lucia	0.770
59. Grenada	0.737
60. Chile	0.713
61. Brazil	0.692
62. Dominica	0.690
63. Argentina	0.687

Table A. 1 (continued)

Country	*Growth Coefficient (Cg) 1990*
64. Uruguay	0.685
65. Romania	0.661
66. Botswana	0.646
67. Cuba	0.629
68. Lebanon	0.583
69. Costa Rica	0.552
70. Malaysia	0.545
71. Suriname	0.540
72. Macedonia, FYR	0.536
73. St. Vincent and the Grenadines	0.535
74. Kazakhstan	0.532
75. Panama	0.532
76. Mauritius	0.526
77. Fiji	0.503
78. Bulgaria	0.495
79. Colombia	0.490
80. Namibia	0.487
81. Ecuador	0.458
82. Ukraine	0.457
83. Belize	0.446
84. Algeria	0.440
85. Georgia	0.432
86. Marshall Islands	0.416
87. Belarus	0.403
88. Turkmenistan	0.379
89. Dominican Republic	0.373
90. Tunisia	0.352
91. Micronesia, Fed.Sts.	0.342
92. Iraq	0.338
93. Peru	0.329
94. Vanuatu	0.318
95. Tonga	0.317
96. Congo. Rep.	0.314
97. El Salvador	0.314
98. Iran, Islamic Republic	0.312
99. Jordan	0.306
100. Samoa	0.306
101. Guatemala	0.305
102. Albania	0.296
103. Tuvalu	0.292
104. Azerbaijan	0.289

(*continued*)

Table A. 1 (continued)

Country	*Growth Coefficient (C_g) 1990*
105. Moldova	0.279
106. Thailand	0.272
107. Angola	0.268
108. Paraguay	0.256
109. Morocco	0.247
110. Djibouti	0.215
111. Armenia	0.198
112. Honduras	0.197
113. Cote d'Ivoire	0.194
114. Syrian Arab Republic	0.192
115. Phillipines	0.173
116. Cameroon	0.173
117. Kiribati	0.171
118. Solomon Islands	0.170
119. Nicaragua	0.162
120. Egypt. Arab Rep.	0.152
121. Mongolia	0.146
122. Indonesia	0.145
123. Bolivia	0.144
124. Tajikistan	0.124
125. Sri Lanka	0.123
126. Cabo Verde	0.122
127. Papua New Guinea	0.122
128. Kyrgyz Republic	0.121
129. Guyana	0.118
130. Senegal	0.118
131. Zimbabwe	0.117
132. Comoros	0.116
133. Zambia	0.115
134. Yemen, Republic	0.115
135. Mauritania	0.114
136. Bhutan	0.111
137. Nigeria	0.102
138. Sudan	0.098
139. Kenya	0.096
140. Uzbekistan	0.095
141. Pakistan	0.091
142. Lesotho	0.088
143. Congo, Dem.Rep.	0.088
144. Guinea Bissau	0.086
145. China	0.080
146. Benin	0.079
147. Togo	0.074

Table A. 1 (continued)

Country	*Growth Coefficient (Cg) 1990*
148. Gambia, The	0.073
149. Chad	0.071
150. India	0.070
151. Equatorial Guinea	0.068
152. Central African Republic	0.065
153. Ghana	0.065
154. Sierra Leone	0.063
155. Tanzania	0.060
156. Mali	0.057
157. Madagascar	0.057
158. Bangladesh	0.055
159. Niger	0.052
160. Vietnam	0.052
161. Guinea	0.049
162. Burkina Faso	0.047
163. Lao PDR	0.045
164. Swaziland	0.045
165. Rwanda	0.042
166. Nepal	0.040
167. Burundi	0.038
168. Uganda	0.034
169. Malawi	0.033
170. Mozambique	0.032
171. Liberia	0.031
172. Ethiopia	0.025
Average TopFive	11.651
Average LowFive	0.031
TopFive/LowFive	**376.3**
Average TopTen	9.387
Average LowTen	0.036
TopTen/LowTen	**257.3**
Average TopTwenty	7.267
Average LowTwenty	0.046
TopTwenty/LowTwenty	**157.4**
Average TopFive (excl. Monaco, Liechtenstein, and Bermuda)	8.193
Average LowFive	0.031
TopFive*/LowFive	**264.6**

Table A. 2 Fastest growing economies in the period 1990–2000

Country	*Percentage change in Cg 2000/1990*
Equatorial Guinea	872.44
Swaziland	634.14
China	110.89
Cabo Verde	104.63
Ireland	59.41
Vietnam	53.45
Korea, Republic	49.29
Isle of Man	43.16
Lebanon	38.66
Chile	38.20
Guyana	36.50
Malta	35.43
Malaysia	34.30
Bhutan	34.10
Liechtenstein	33.93
Dominican Republic	31.02
Singapore	30.87
Israel	30.45
Mauritius	30.37
San Marino	29.30
Sri Lanka	28.75
Poland	25.51
Tuvalu	24.73
Lao PDR	24.70
India	24.70
Luxembourg	24.49
El Salvador	22.29
Thailand	22.01
Belize	21.50
Argentina	19.88
Uganda	18.08
Tunisia	17.92
Norway	17.84
Panama	15.96
St. Kitts and Nevis	15.46
St. Vincent and the Grenadines	15.30
Trinidad and Tobago	14.43
Seychelles	13.85
Uruguay	13.78
Costa Rica	13.39
Egypt, Arab Rep.	12.74

Table A. 2 (continued)

Country	*Percentage change in Cg 2000/1990*
Oman	12.67
Indonesia	12.37
Portugal	12.07
Tonga	11.88
Puerto Rico	11.74
Netherlands	11.61
Grenada	11.42
Bangladesh	11.40
Burkina Faso	10.72
Bahrain	10.72
Nepal	10.54
Spain	10.43
Botswana	10.38
Mozambique	9.71
Hong Kong, SAR China	9.64
Denmark	8.98
Lesotho	8.81
Bermuda	8.74
Syrian Arab Republic	8.56
St. Lucia	8.52
Austria	7.91
United States	7.86
Sudan	7.77
Australia	7.14
Iran, Islamic Republic	7.11
United Kingdom	7.06
Peru	6.78
Cyprus	6.67
Turkey	6.12
Albania	6.01
Belgium	5.58
Dominica	5.31
Finland	4.92
Kiribati	4.11
Canada	4.09
Greenland	3.68
Sweden	3.57
Guatemala	3.25
Greece	3.20
Ghana	2.93
Samoa	2.90

(*continued*)

Table A. 2 (continued)

Country	*Percentage change in Cg 2000/1990*
France	2.56
Mexico	2.43
Germany	2.06
Iceland	2.04
Italy	1.99
Malawi	1.73
Yemen. Rep.	1.48
New Zealand	1.19
Bolivia	0.65
Papua New Guinea	0.41
Mali	0.29
Micronesia, Fed.Sts.	-0.66
Morocco	-1.10
Pakistan	-1.18
Nicaragua	-1.58
Andorra	-1.63
Fiji	-1.72
Barbados	-1.83
Antigua and Barbuda	-2.41
Benin	-2.61
Vanuatu	-3.29
Brazil	-3.56
Monaco	-4.16
Jordan	-5.22
Japan	-5.29
Honduras	-5.53
Colombia	-5.64
Macao, SAR China	-5.72
Namibia	-7.10
Bahamas, The	-7.62
Czech Republic	-7.97
Phillipines	-8.03
Switzerland	-8.43
Saudi Arabia	-8.56
Iraq	-8.78
Senegal	-10.26
Gambia, The	-10.29
Tanzania	-12.10
Guinea	-12.21
Paraguay	-12.40
Zimbabwe	-13.45

Table A. 2 (continued)

Country	*Percentage change in Cg 2000/1990*
Venezuela, RB	-13.54
Marshall Islands	-13.78
Ecuador	-14.19
Algeria	-15.02
Mauritania	-15.03
Bulgaria	-15.47
Solomon Islands	-15.73
Togo	-15.98
Brunei Darussalam	-16.03
South Africa	-16.73
Ethiopia	-17.00
Cote d'Ivoire	--18.03
Liberia	-18.09
United Arab Emirates	-18.22
Nigeria	-18.65
Suriname	-18.92
Zambia	-20.46
Gabon	-20.83
Mongolia	-21.01
Belarus	-21.50
Kenya	-21.58
Central African Republic	-21.77
Chad	-21.93
Macedonia, FYR	-22.33
Rwanda	-22.41
Congo, Republic	-23.66
Comoros	-23.93
Madagascar	-24.30
Romania	-24.30
Cameroon	-24.51
Guinea Bissau	-26.16
Niger	-26.81
Cuba	-28.34
Uzbekistan	-29.13
Angola	-30.41
Armenia	-32.07
Kazakhstan	-33.71
Sierra Leone	-34.44
Burundi	-40.16
Djibouti	-40.77
Russian Federation	-40.82

(*continued*)

Table A. 2 (continued)

Country	*Percentage change in Cg 2000/1990*
Turkmenistan	–44.31
Kyrgyz Republic	–48.10
Azerbaijan	–54.47
Ukraine	–60.15
Congo, Dem.Rep.	–63.67
Georgia	–64.56
Moldova	–68.57
Tajikistan	–71.64

Source: Author's calculations based on World Bank data.

Table A. 3 Fastest growing economies in the period 2000–2009

Country	*Percentage change in Cg 2009/2000*
Azerbaijan	202.90
Equatorial Guinea	174.44
China	109.71
Armenia	96.20
Angola	87.16
Belarus	79.51
Macao, SAR China	78.19
Kazakhstan	71.92
Chad	59.95
Cambodia	58.56
Turkmenistan	56.59
Georgia	55.44
Nigeria	54.79
Tajikistan	54.12
Romania	53.10
Albania	52.68
Latvia	51.79
Trinidad and Tobago	49.28
Bhutan	48.35
India	47.62
Bulgaria	45.81
Vietnam	44.79
Uzbekistan	44.59
Cuba	44.14
Rwanda	42.71

Table A. 3 (continued)

Country	*Percentage change in Cg 2009/2000*
Ethiopia	42.58
Mongolia	42.34
Lao PDR	41.97
Russian Federation	41.80
Serbia	41.70
Cabo Verde	41.67
Moldova	41.60
Ukraine	40.42
Mozambique	38.03
Slovak Republic	37.89
Sudan	33.48
Bosnia and Herzegovina	32.55
Zambia	31.90
Jordan	31.59
Bangladesh	29.95
Panama	29.74
Morocco	29.04
Sri Lanka	28.92
Uganda	28.83
Peru	28.42
Estonia	27.92
Poland	26.81
Tanzania	25.57
Suriname	25.08
Korea, Rep.	24.60
Indonesia	24.23
Iran, Islamic Rep.	23.91
Kyrgyz Republic	23.18
Tunisia	22.93
St. Vincent and the Grenadines	22.88
Montenegro	22.72
Liberia	22.47
Hong Kong, SAR China	20.17
Thailand	20.05
Namibia	19.29
Mauritius	19.25
Egypt, Arab Rep.	18.43
Czech Republic	18.18
Dominican Republic	17.33
Burkina Faso	16.96
Croatia	16.77

(*continued*)

Table A. 3 (continued)

Country	*Percentage change in Cg 2009/2000*
Sierra Leone	16.76
Ghana	16.24
Libya	15.88
Lesotho	15.63
Monaco	15.50
Mali	15.07
Dominica	15.07
Macedonia, FYR	14.09
Pakistan	13.12
Sao Tome and Principe	13.11
Chile	12.95
Samoa	12.90
Timor-Leste	12.78
Slovenia	12.76
Phillipines	12.60
Colombia	12.51
Lebanon	12.38
Djibouti	12.22
Costa Rica	12.22
Algeria	11.93
Botswana	11.37
Uruguay	11.28
Hungary	11.08
Singapore	10.94
Malaysia	10.87
Greece	10.75
Ecuador	10.62
Argentina	10.62
Nepal	10.17
Honduras	8.62
Brazil	8.05
South Africa	7.99
Iceland	7.25
Bolivia	7.17
Turkey	6.95
Mauritania	6.36
Saudi Arabia	6.25
Venezuela, RB	6.23
Grenada	5.93
Antigua and Barbuda	5.25
Australia	5.18

Table A. 3 (continued)

Country	*Percentage change in Cg 2009/2000*
Cyprus	3.21
El Salvador	3.20
Congo, Dem.Rep.	3.05
Nicaragua	2.48
New Zealand	2.17
Congo, Rep.	2.02
Belize	1.86
St. Kitts and Nevis	1.69
Marshall Islands	1.68
Malawi	1.54
Senegal	1.18
San Marino	1.14
Yemen, Rep.	0.74
Andorra	0.50
Swaziland	0.42
Bermuda	0.35
Finland	0.33
Sweden	−0.15
Papua New Guinea	−0.26
Kenya	−0.35
Israel	−0.56
United Kingdom	−0.81
Austria	−1.46
Greenland	−1.47
Qatar	−1.52
Netherlands	−1.70
Oman	−2.14
Puerto Rico	−2.41
Switzerland	−2.43
Luxembourg	−2.46
Spain	−2.61
Guatemala	−2.61
Fiji	−2.64
Norway	−2.80
St. Lucia	−2.81
Liechtenstein	−2.93
Kuwait	−2.99
Benin	−3.11
Belgium	−3.14
Seychelles	−3.28
Ireland	−3.32

(*continued*)

Table A. 3 (continued)

Country	*Percentage change in Cg 2009/2000*
Canada	–3.74
Cameroon	–4.32
United States	–4.90
Germany	–5.01
Guyana	–5.15
Central African Republic	–5.39
Vanuatu	–5.55
Guinea	–5.58
Paraguay	–5.82
Barbados	–5.98
France	–6.21
Malta	–6.28
Niger	–6.67
Gambia. The	–6.99
Tonga	–7.05
Portugal	–7.36
Comoros	–7.48
Japan	–8.01
Micronesia, Fed.Sts.	–8.10
Denmark	–8.19
Iraq	–8.19
Mexico	–8.77
Guinea Bissau	–9.18
Burundi	–9.98
West Bank and Gaza	–10.33
Solomon Islands	–11.08
Madagascar	–11.16
Kiribati	–11.80
Italy	–11.96
Tuvalu	–12.62
Cote d'Ivoire	–14.57
Togo	–15.11
Brunei Darussalam	–15.30
Haiti	–15.44
Palau	–15.48
Bahrain	–18.47
Bahamas, The	–19.89
Gabon	–22.12
Aruba	–24.53
Eritrea	–31.82
United Arab Emirates	–49.19
Zimbabwe	–51.68

Source: The author's calculations based on World Bank data

Table A. 4 Fastest growing economies in the period 2000–2014

Country	*Percentage change in Cg – 2014/2000*
1. Azerbaijan	212.00
2. China	185.38
3. Macao, SAR China	178.34
4. Turkmenistan	129.68
5. Armenia	121.44
6. Equatorial Guinea	117.72
7. Mongolia	105.83
8. Kazakhstan	98.07
9. Belarus	97.86
10. Ethiopia	91.32
11. Cambodia	88.21
12. Angola	85.46
13. Georgia	84.22
14. India	81.79
15. Uzbekistan	79.18
16. Chad	78.59
17. Tajikistan	77.77
18. Lao PDR	76.23
19. Bhutan	73.27
20. Latvia	72.26
21. Moldova	69.99
22. Sri Lanka	69.05
23. Vietnam	68.72
24. Nigeria	64.58
25. Liberia	64.38
26. Panama	64.23
27. Sierra Leone	62.11
28. Rwanda	61.83
29. Albania	59.48
30. Mozambique	59.30
31. Romania	55.05
32. Bangladesh	52.59
33. Russian Federation	49.53
34. Cuba	48.74
35. Peru	47.81
36. Zambia	47.39
37. Bulgaria	47.22
38. Ghana	44.78
39. Estonia	44.70
40. Slovak Republic	43.93
41. Indonesia	43.02

(*continued*)

Table A. 4 (continued)

Country	*Percentage change in Cg – 2014/2000*
42. Cabo Verde	39.77
43. Tanzania	38.16
44. Trinidad and Tobago	38.14
45. Timor-Leste	37.10
46. Poland	36.90
47. Serbia	36.76
48. Botswana	35.77
49. Ukraine	34.88
50. Korea. Republic	34.88
51. Morocco	33.20
52. Uganda	30.95
53. Dominican Republic	30.85
54. Thailand	30.26
55. Mauritius	30.08
56. Suriname	29.67
57. Namibia	29.49
58. Phillipines	29.46
59. Uruguay	28.80
60. Bosnia and Herzegovina	28.61
61. Hong Kong, SAR China	28.60
62. Burkina Faso	27.86
63. Lesotho	27.44
64. Singapore	27.23
65. Kyrgyz Republic	27.19
66. Chile	25.13
67. Malaysia	25.07
68. Jordan	24.38
69. Colombia	23.15
70. Montenegro	21.89
71. Argentina	21.01
72. Djibouti	20.88
73. Turkey	20.69
74. Congo, Dem.Rep.	20.51
75. Ecuador	20.49
76. Nepal	19.60
77. Costa Rica	19.37
78. Tunisia	18.90
79. Bolivia	18.30
80. Macedonia, FYR	17.89
81. Sudan	17.17
82. Saudi Arabia	15.56

Table A. 4 (continued)

Country	*Percentage change in Cg – 2014/2000*
83. Egypt, Arab Rep.	15.07
84. Pakistan	14.25
85. Czech Republic	13.73
86. Lebanon	13.34
87. Mauritania	13.07
88. Sao Tome and Principe	12.91
89. Papua New Guinea	12.40
90. Seychelles	12.22
91. Brazil	11.95
92. St. Vincent and the Grenadines	11.90
93. Nicaragua	11.20
94. Hungary	10.99
95. Algeria	10.98
96. Paraguay	10.91
97. Iran, Islamic Rep.	10.63
98. Mali	8.44
99. Kenya	7.82
100. Guyana	7.33
101. Croatia	6.76
102. Samoa	6.56
103. Congo, Republic	6.32
104. Marshall Islands	6.05
105. Dominica	5.84
106. South Africa	4.38
107. Slovenia	3.89
108. Malawi	2.35
109. Australia	2.06
110. Iceland	1.97
111. El Salvador	1.14
112. Israel	0.85
113. Honduras	0.73
114. Fiji	-0.02
115. Sweden	-0.45
116. Iraq	-0.80
117. Qatar	-0.90
118. Grenada	-1.05
119. Niger	-1.28
120. Cameroon	-2.04
121. Germany	-2.13
122. New Zealand	-2.17
123. Solomon Islands	-2.52
124. Benin	-2.94
125. United Kingdom	-3.78

(*continued*)

Table A. 4 (continued)

Country	*Percentage change in Cg – 2014/2000*
126. Venezuela, RB	-4.06
127. Swaziland	-4.07
128. Senegal	-4.19
129. Canada	-4.48
130. St. Kitts and Nevis	-4.72
131. Austria	-5.17
132. Guatemala	-5.31
133. United States	-5.65
134. Ireland	-5.78
135. Mexico	-6.61
136. Finland	-6.99
137. Belize	-7.32
138. Japan	-7.85
139. Switzerland	-7.90
140. Malta	-8.03
141. Belgium	-9.01
142. Norway	-9.20
143. Cote d'Ivoire	-9.25
144. Palau	-9.52
145. Netherlands	-9.75
146. Antigua and Barbuda	-9.92
147. Tonga	-10.37
148. France	-10.90
149. Luxembourg	-11.29
150. Tuvalu	-11.37
151. Togo	-11.49
151. Puerto Rico	-12.18
152. Spain	-12.34
153. Burundi	-12.76
154. Comoros	-12.79
155. Guinea	-13.81
156. Micronesia, Fed.States	-14.35
157. Denmark	-14.59
158. Guinea Bissau	-14.60
159. West Bank and Gaza	-14.87
160. Kuwait	-14.93
161. Gabon	-15.38
162. Kiribati	-15.94
163. Vanuatu	-16.46
164. Portugal	-17.04
165. Cyprus	-17.14
166. Gambia, The	-17.22
167. Bermuda	-17.29

Table A. 4 (continued)

Country	*Percentage change in Cg – 2014/2000*
168. St. Lucia	-17.40
169. Greece	-18.51
170. Bahrain	-18.81
171. Andorra	-18.86
172. Brunei Darussalam	-19.19
173. Haiti	-19.81
174. Madagascar	-21.09
175. Yemen, Republic	-22.38
176. Italy	-23.44
177. Barbados	-27.28
178. Bahamas, The	-27.78
179. Oman	-29.23
180. Eritrea	-34.33
181. Zimbabwe	-41.44
182. Central African Republic	-43.29
183. Libya	-45.36
184. United Arab Emirates	-53.33

Source: The author's calculation based on World Bank data.

Table A. 5 Ranking by the size of growth coefficient in 2014

Country	*Growth coefficient 2014*
1. Luxembourg	9.731
2. Bermuda	8.597
3. Norway	8.422
4. Qatar	7.614
5. Iceland	7.466
6. Switzerland	7.298
7. Macao, SAR China	6.577
8. Ireland	6.181
9. Denmark	5.954
10. United States	5.812
11. Sweden	5.768
12. Netherlands	5.403
13. Austria	5.145
14. United Kingdom	5.131
15. Germany	4.974
16. Finland	4.863

(*continued*)

Table A. 5 (continued)

Country	*Growth coefficient 2014*
17. Canada	4.796
18. Singapore	4.770
19. Belgium	4.741
20. Australia	4.737
21. Japan	4.708
22. France	4.467
23. Hong Kong, SAR China	4.286
24. Andorra	4.139
25. Kuwait	3.656
26. New Zealand	3.602
27. Italy	3.567
28. United Arab Emirates	3.228
29. Spain	3.208
30. Brunei Darussalam	3.150
31. Korea, Rep.	3.076
32. Israel	3.073
33. Bahamas, The	2.588
34. Puerto Rico	2.513
35. Slovenia	2.394
36. Greece	2.301
37. Portugal	2.292
38. Bahrain	2.270
39. Saudi Arabia	2.232
40. Malta	2.081
41. Cyprus	2.027
42. Slovak Republic	1.969
43. Seychelles	1.943
44. Czech Republic	1.871
45. Trinidad and Tobago	1.784
46. Estonia	1.546
47. Barbados	1.511
48. Hungary	1.489
49. Antigua and Barbuda	1.470
50. Equatorial Guinea	1.450
51. Oman	1.445
52. St. Kitts and Nevis	1.421
53. Poland	1.416
54. Lithuania	1.387
55. Croatia	1.323
56. Latvia	1.249
57. Chile	1.233
58. Palau	1.175
59. Turkey	1.111

Table A. 5 (continued)

Country	*Growth coefficient 2014*
60. Mexico	1.080
61. Panama	1.013
62. Uruguay	1.004
63. Argentina	0.996
64. Botswana	0.967
65. Lebanon	0.916
66. Malaysia	0.915
67. Gabon	0.901
68. Mauritius	0.891
69. Russian Federation	0.871
70. Grenada	0.813
71. Romania	0.776
72. Maldives	0.770
73. Dominica	0.769
74. South Africa	0.762
75. Venezuela. RB	0.759
76. Brazil	0.748
77. Costa Rica	0.747
78. Kazakhstan	0.698
79. St. Vincent and the Grenadines	0.691
80. St. Lucia	0.690
81. Cuba	0.671
82. Dominican Republic	0.639
83. Belarus	0.626
84. Bulgaria	0.616
85. Montenegro	0.596
86. Namibia	0.586
87. Libya	0.585
88. Colombia	0.570
89. Suriname	0.567
90. Serbia	0.532
91. Peru	0.520
92. Belize	0.502
93. Albania	0.500
94. Fiji	0.494
95. Tunisia	0.493
96. Macedonia, FYR	0.491
97. Turkmenistan	0.485
98. China	0.484
99. Ecuador	0.474
100. Thailand	0.432
101. Bosnia and Herzegovina	0.432
102. Algeria	0.415

(*continued*)

Table A. 5 (continued)

Country	*Growth coefficient 2014*
103. Azerbaijan	0.410
104. El Salvador	0.389
105. Marshall Islands	0.380
106. Iran, Islamic Rep.	0.369
107. Jordan	0.360
108. Cabo Verde	0.350
109. Angola	0.346
110. Samoa	0.335
111. Morocco	0.326
112. Tuvalu	0.323
113. Tonga	0.318
114. Swaziland	0.316
115. Iraq	0.305
116. Armenia	0.298
117. Guatemala	0.298
118. Micronesia, Fed.States	0.291
119. Georgia	0.282
120. Sri Lanka	0.267
121. Bhutan	0.259
122. Vanuatu	0.257
123. Congo, Republic	0.255
124. Paraguay	0.248
125. Ukraine	0.246
126. Mongolia	0.238
127. Indonesia	0.234
128. Phillipines	0.207
129. Egypt, Arab Rep.	0.197
130. Honduras	0.187
131. Nicaragua	0.177
132. West Bank and Gaza	0.174
133. Guyana	0.173
134. Bolivia	0.172
135. India	0.158
136. Djibouti	0.154
137. Kiribati	0.149
138. Moldova	0.149
139. Cote d'Ivoire	0.145
140. Solomon Islands	0.140
141. Papua New Guinea	0.137
142. Nigeria	0.137
143. Zambia	0.135

Table A. 5 (continued)

Country	*Growth coefficient 2014*
144. Vietnam	0.135
145. Cameroon	0.128
146. Sao Tome and Principe	0.126
147. Sudan	0.124
148. Lesotho	0.123
149. Uzbekistan	0.120
150. Mauritania	0.109
151. Timor-Leste	0.105
152. Pakistan	0.103
153. Senegal	0.101
154. Lao PDR	0.099
155. Chad	0.099
156. Ghana	0.097
157. Bangladesh	0.094
158. Cambodia	0.093
159. Yemen, Rep.	0.091
160. Kenya	0.081
161. Kyrgyz Republic	0.080
162. Comoros	0.077
163. Benin	0.075
164. Tanzania	0.073
165. Sierra Leone	0.067
166. Burkina Faso	0.066
167. Tajikistan	0.063
168. Haiti	0.062
169. Mali	0.062
170. Zimbabwe	0.060
171. Mozambique	0.057
172. Togo	0.055
173. Gambia, The	0.055
174. Guinea Bissau	0.054
175. Nepal	0.053
176. Uganda	0.053
178. Rwanda	0.052
179. Afghanistan	0.052
180. Liberia	0.041
181. Ethiopia	0.040
182. Congo, Dem.Rep.	0.038
183. Niger	0.038
184. Guinea	0.037
185. Malawi	0.034

(*continued*)

Table A. 5 (continued)

Country	*Growth coefficient 2014*
186. Madagascar	0.034
187. Central African Republic	0.029
188. Eritrea	0.024
189. Burundi	0.020
Average TopFive	8.366
Average LowestFive	0.0282
TopFive/LowFive	**296.7**
Average TopTen	7.365
Average LowestTen	0.034
TopTen/LowestTen	**219.6**
Average TopTwenty	6.199
Average LowestTwenty	0.044
TopTwenty/LowestTwenty	**139.7**

Source: The author's calculation based on World Bank data.

Table A. 6 Fastest growing economies in the world: 2009–2014

Country	*Percentage change in Cg 2009–2014*
Macao, SAR China	56.20
Turkmenistan	46.68
Mongolia	44.60
Sierra Leone	38.84
China	36.08
Liberia	34.21
Ethiopia	34.19
Sri Lanka	31.13
Panama	26.58
Ghana	24.55
Lao PDR	24.13
Uzbekistan	23.92
India	23.14
Botswana	21.92
Timor-Leste	21.56
Zimbabwe	21.21
Moldova	20.05
Lithuania	18.81

Table A. 6 (continued)

Country	*Percentage change in Cg 2009–2014*
Cambodia	18.70
Georgia	18.51
Paraguay	17.76
Bangladesh	17.42
Maldives	17.39
Congo, Dem.Rep.	16.94
Bhutan	16.80
Vietnam	16.52
Seychelles	16.03
Uruguay	15.74
Mozambique	15.41
Tajikistan	15.35
Kazakhstan	15.21
Indonesia	15.13
Peru	15.10
Phillipines	14.98
Singapore	14.68
Latvia	13.48
Rwanda	13.40
Guyana	13.15
Estonia	13.11
Armenia	12.86
Turkey	12.85
Malaysia	12.81
Papua New Guinea	12.69
Afghanistan	12.08
Zambia	11.75
Chad	11.65
Dominican Republic	11.53
Chile	10.78
Bolivia	10.38
Belarus	10.22
Lesotho	10.21
Tanzania	10.02
Solomon Islands	9.63
Colombia	9.46
Argentina	9.39
Burkina Faso	9.32
Mauritius	9.08
Ecuador	8.91
Saudi Arabia	8.76

(*continued*)

Table A. 6 (continued)

Country	*Percentage change in Cg 2009–2014*
Gabon	8.65
Nepal	8.56
Namibia	8.56
Nicaragua	8.51
Thailand	8.50
Korea, Rep.	8.25
Kenya	8.20
Iraq	8.05
Poland	7.96
Djibouti	7.71
Palau	7.05
Hong Kong, SAR China	7.01
Costa Rica	6.37
Nigeria	6.32
Mauritania	6.31
Cote d'Ivoire	6.23
Niger	5.78
Russian Federation	5.45
Albania	4.45
Slovak Republic	4.38
Marshall Islands	4.29
Togo	4.26
Congo, Rep.	4.22
Suriname	3.67
Brazil	3.61
Macedonia, FYR	3.34
Kyrgyz Republic	3.26
Morocco	3.23
Cuba	3.19
Germany	3.03
Azerbaijan	3.00
Fiji	2.70
Cameroon	2.39
Mexico	2.38
Uganda	1.64
Tuvalu	1.43
Israel	1.42
Romania	1.28
Pakistan	1.01
Bulgaria	0.97
Lebanon	0.86

Table A. 6 (continued)

Country	*Percentage change in Cg 2009–2014*
Malawi	0.79
Qatar	0.64
Japan	0.18
Benin	0.17
Hungary	−0.08
Sao Tome and Principe	−0.18
Sweden	−0.30
Bahrain	−0.41
Montenegro	−0.67
Canada	−0.77
United States	−0.79
Algeria	−0.84
Angola	−0.90
Cabo Verde	−1.35
Malta	−1.87
El Salvador	−1.99
Ireland	−2.54
Guatemala	−2.77
Egypt, Arab Rep.	−2.84
Australia	−2.97
Bosnia and Herzegovina	−2.97
United Kingdom	−2.99
Burundi	−3.09
Tunisia	−3.28
South Africa	−3.35
Serbia	−3.49
Tonga	−3.58
Eritrea	−3.69
Austria	−3.76
Czech Republic	−3.77
Ukraine	−3.94
New Zealand	−4.25
Swaziland	−4.47
Brunei Darussalam	−4.59
Kiribati	−4.68
Iceland	−4.93
France	−5.01
West Bank and Gaza	−5.06
Haiti	−5.17
Senegal	−5.31
Jordan	−5.48

(*continued*)

Table A. 6 (continued)

Country	*Percentage change in Cg 2009–2014*
Switzerland	-5.61
Samoa	-5.61
Comoros	-5.75
Mali	-5.76
Guinea Bissau	-5.97
Belgium	-6.05
St. Kitts and Nevis	-6.30
Norway	-6.58
Grenada	-6.60
Micronesia, Fed.Sts.	-6.80
Denmark	-6.97
Honduras	-7.26
Finland	-7.30
Trinidad and Tobago	-7.46
Slovenia	-7.87
Dominica	-8.02
United Arab Emirates	-8.15
Netherlands	-8.20
Croatia	-8.58
Guinea	-8.71
St. Vincent and the Grenadines	-8.93
Belize	-9.02
Luxembourg	-9.05
Venezuela, RB	-9.69
Bahamas, The	-9.85
Spain	-10.00
Puerto Rico	-10.01
Portugal	-10.45
Iran. Islamic Rep.	-10.72
Gambia, The	-11.00
Madagascar	-11.18
Vanuatu	-11.56
Sudan	-12.22
Kuwait	-12.31
Italy	-13.29
Antigua and Barbuda	-14.41
St. Lucia	-15.02
Bermuda	-17.58
Andorra	-19.26
Cyprus	-19.71
Equatorial Guinea	-20.67

Table A. 6 (continued)

Country	*Percentage change in Cg 2009–2014*
Barbados	-22.65
Yemen, Rep.	-22.95
Greece	-26.42
Oman	-27.68
Central African Republic	-40.06
Libya	-52.85

Source: The author's calculation based on World Bank data.

Table A. 7 Fastest growing economies in the 2000–2005 and 2005–2009

Country	*Percentage change in Cg 2005/2000*	*Country*	*Percentage change in Cg 2009/2005*
Equatorial Guinea	183.51	Azerbaijan	81.84
Armenia	67.39	China	47.33
Chad	66.65	Angola	47.23
Azerbaijan	66.58	Turkmenistan	39.64
Kazakhstan	48.46	Liberia	33.50
Macao, SAR China	47.98	Afghanistan	31.87
Latvia	46.06	Belarus	30.90
China	42.34	Ethiopia	30.52
Ukraine	39.34	Uzbekistan	27.86
Belarus	37.14	Bhutan	26.72
Nigeria	34.34	Cabo Verde	26.02
Estonia	34.23	Maldives	25.74
Tajikistan	33.69	Panama	25.49
Georgia	33.11	India	25.02
Trinidad and Tobago	32.42	Timor-Leste	24.10
Cambodia	31.93	Albania	24.07
Moldova	31.46	Cuba	23.99
Romania	28.99	Lebanon	22.60
Angola	27.12	Lao PDR	22.18
Russian Federation	26.88	Monaco	22.09
Serbia	25.93	Rwanda	21.43
Bulgaria	25.62	Sudan	20.87
Albania	23.07	Macao, SAR China	20.41
Mozambique	22.46	Peru	20.39

(*continued*)

Table A. 7 (continued)

Country	*Percentage change in Cg 2005/2000*	*Country*	*Percentage change in Cg 2009/2005*
Vietnam	21.33	Cambodia	20.19
Mongolia	19.79	Zambia	20.17
Slovak Republic	18.32	Uruguay	19.72
India	18.08	Uganda	19.49
Rwanda	17.52	Vietnam	19.34
Isle of Man	17.35	Bangladesh	18.88
Bhutan	17.06	Mongolia	18.83
Cuba	16.25	Romania	18.68
Lao PDR	16.20	Poland	18.47
Bosnia and Herzegovina	16.10	Sri Lanka	18.30
Hungary	14.77	Jordan	18.11
Croatia	14.51	Montenegro	17.54
Tanzania	14.48	Armenia	17.21
Samoa	14.19	Egypt, Arab Rep.	17.15
Grenada	13.99	Kyrgyz Republic	16.90
Suriname	13.82	Oman	16.85
Iran, Islamic Rep.	13.77	Georgia	16.77
St. Vincent and the Grenadines	13.69	Slovak Republic	16.55
Kuwait	13.65	Bulgaria	16.07
Korea, Rep.	13.51	Kazakhstan	15.81
Uzbekistan	13.09	Dominica	15.57
Algeria	12.70	Dominican Republic	15.34
Thailand	12.50	Tajikistan	15.28
Cabo Verde	12.42	Nigeria	15.22
Czech Republic	12.31	Morocco	15.12
Turkmenistan	12.14	Mauritius	15.05
Morocco	12.09	Indonesia	14.84
Jordan	11.41	Sao Tome and Principe	14.50
Hong Kong, SAR China	10.98	Malawi	14.31
Singapore	10.56	Macedonia, FYR	14.25
Sudan	10.43	Tunisia	14.22
Namibia	9.88	Bosnia and Herzegovina	14.17
Zambia	9.76	Argentina	13.79
Greece	9.71	Lesotho	12.86
Libya	9.68	Djibouti	12.85
Slovenia	9.46	Trinidad and Tobago	12.73
Bangladesh	9.32	Mozambique	12.71
Ethiopia	9.24	Serbia	12.52

Table A. 7 (continued)

Country	*Percentage change in Cg 2005/2000*	*Country*	*Percentage change in Cg 2009/2005*
Andorra	9.09	Ghana	11.96
Sri Lanka	8.98	Russian Federation	11.76
Burkina Faso	8.64	Iraq	11.63
Indonesia	8.17	Venezuela, RB	11.16
Uganda	7.82	Saudi Arabia	11.14
Mali	7.77	Vanuatu	10.69
Tunisia	7.62	Colombia	10.51
Turkey	7.48	Nepal	10.29
Chile	7.21	Papua New Guinea	10.09
Iceland	7.20	Sierra Leone	9.90
Pakistan	7.17	Suriname	9.89
Poland	7.04	Bolivia	9.88
Ireland	6.97	Korea, Rep.	9.77
Peru	6.67	Tanzania	9.69
Puerto Rico	6.50	Costa Rica	9.45
Ecuador	6.35	Seychelles	8.95
Sierra Leone	6.24	Iran, Islamic Rep.	8.91
Syrian Arab Republic	5.77	Namibia	8.56
Malaysia	5.38	Brazil	8.49
Kyrgyz Republic	5.38	Hong Kong, SAR China	8.28
Belize	5.00	St. Vincent and the Grenadines	8.08
New Zealand	4.91	Botswana	8.02
Honduras	4.67	Phillipines	7.79
Phillipines	4.46	Moldova	7.71
Montenegro	4.40	Burkina Faso	7.66
United Kingdom	3.94	Liechtenstein	7.22
Ghana	3.83	Israel	7.15
Palau	3.67	Lithuania	6.99
Mauritius	3.65	Mauritania	6.84
South Africa	3.46	Mali	6.77
Finland	3.43	Thailand	6.71
Panama	3.39	Congo. Dem.Rep.	6.64
Sweden	3.19	Libya	5.65
St. Kitts and Nevis	3.12	Pakistan	5.55
Botswana	3.10	Chile	5.36
Fiji	2.74	Czech Republic	5.22
Marshall Islands	2.66	Malaysia	5.21
Costa Rica	2.53	Tuvalu	4.86

(*continued*)

Table A. 7 (continued)

Country	*Percentage change in Cg 2005/2000*	*Country*	*Percentage change in Cg 2009/2005*
Lesotho	2.45	South Africa	4.38
Antigua and Barbuda	2.17	Solomon Islands	4.16
Colombia	1.81	Ecuador	4.02
Dominican Republic	1.72	Greenland	3.93
El Salvador	1.67	Latvia	3.92
Australia	1.63	Honduras	3.77
Bermuda	1.55	Australia	3.49
Senegal	1.36	San Marino	3.48
Egypt, Arab Rep.	1.10	Kenya	3.35
Nicaragua	0.75	St. Lucia	3.27
Luxembourg	0.73	Malta	3.05
Spain	0.52	Antigua and Barbuda	3.01
Tonga	0.36	Slovenia	3.01
Cyprus	0.33	Netherlands	2.93
Norway	-0.08	Guatemala	2.92
Nepal	-0.10	Cyprus	2.87
Macedonia, FYR	-0.14	Congo, Rep.	2.71
United States	-0.18	Paraguay	2.49
Brazil	-0.40	Yemen, Rep.	2.14
Canada	-0.41	Central African Republic	2.07
Dominica	-0.44	Burundi	2.02
Mauritania	-0.45	Croatia	1.97
Djibouti	-0.56	Swaziland	1.85
Congo, Rep.	-0.67	Haiti	1.72
Comoros	-0.97	Nicaragua	1.71
West Bank and Gaza	-1.16	Switzerland	1.66
Sao Tome and Principe	-1.21	Gambia, The	1.64
Yemen, Rep.	-1.37	El Salvador	1.50
Swaziland	-1.41	Guyana	1.47
Belgium	-1.65	Benin	1.16
Guinea	-2.00	Greece	0.95
Quatar	-2.01	Guinea Bissau	0.79
Austria	-2.18	Ukraine	0.77
San Marino	-2.26	Austria	0.73
Bolivia	-2.46	Qatar	0.50
Argentina	-2.78	Germany	0.40
Denmark	-2.81	Singapore	0.34
Japan	-2.81	Iceland	0.05
Cameroon	-2.82	Madagascar	-0.03

Table A. 7 (continued)

Country	*Percentage change in Cg 2005/2000*	*Country*	*Percentage change in Cg 2009/2005*
Congo, Dem.Rep.	-3.36	Niger	-0.13
France	-3.45	Cote d'Ivoire	-0.14
Kenya	-3.58	Senegal	-0.18
Micronesia, Fed.Sts.	-3.80	Turkey	-0.49
Switzerland	-4.02	Algeria	-0.69
Benin	-4.22	Togo	-0.85
Saudi Arabia	-4.40	Barbados	-0.89
Venezuela, RB	-4.44	Marshall Islands	-0.95
Netherlands	-4.50	Samoa	-1.14
Italy	-5.05	Bermuda	-1.19
Barbados	-5.13	St. Kitts and Nevis	-1.39
Greenland	-5.19	Belgium	-1.52
Guatemala	-5.38	Cameroon	-1.55
Germany	-5.38	Portugal	-1.82
Monaco	-5.40	New Zealand	-2.61
Portugal	-5.64	Norway	-2.72
St. Lucia	-5.88	Mexico	-2.81
Mexico	-6.13	France	-2.85
Guyana	-6.53	Belize	-2.99
Niger	-6.55	Finland	-2.99
Uruguay	-7.04	Kiribati	-3.09
Israel	-7.20	Spain	-3.12
Central African Republic	-7.31	Luxembourg	-3.17
Brunei Darussalam	-7.79	Equatorial Guinea	-3.20
Paraguay	-8.11	Hungary	-3.21
Liberia	-8.26	Sweden	-3.23
Lebanon	-8.34	Canada	-3.34
Gambia, The	-8.49	Guinea	-3.66
Kiribati	-8.99	Chad	-4.02
Malta	-9.06	Micronesia. Fed.Sts.	-4.47
Timor-Leste	-9.12	United Kingdom	-4.57
Bahamas, The	-9.30	Estonia	-4.70
Papua New Guinea	-9.40	United States	-4.73
Liechtenstein	-9.46	Fiji	-5.24
Guinea Bissau	-9.89	Japan	-5.35
Aruba	-9.91	Denmark	-5.53
Bahrain	-9.94	Comoros	-6.57
Gabon	-10.62	Grenada	-7.06
Madagascar	-11.13	Italy	-7.29

(*continued*)

Table A. 7 (continued)

Country	*Percentage change in Cg 2005/2000*	*Country*	*Percentage change in Cg 2009/2005*
Malawi	-11.17	Tonga	-7.38
Seychelles	-11.23	Andorra	-7.88
Burundi	-11.76	Brunei Darussalam	-8.15
United Arab Emirates	-12.65	Puerto Rico	-8.37
Togo	-14.37	West Bank and Gaza	-9.27
Cote d'Ivoire	-14.45	Bahrain	-9.47
Solomon Islands	-14.63	Ireland	-9.62
Vanuatu	-14.67	Bahamas, The	-11.68
Eritrea	-15.09	Gabon	-12.86
Oman	-16.25	Kuwait	-14.64
Tuvalu	-16.67	Aruba	-16.23
Haiti	-16.87	Palau	-18.47
Iraq	-17.76	Eritrea	-19.71
Zimbabwe	-38.17	Zimbabwe	-21.85
–	–	United Arab Emirates	-41.84

Source: The author's calculations based on World Bank data.

Table A. 8 Fastest growing economies in the period 1990–2014

Country	*Change in Cg 2014/1990*
Equatorial Guinea	2017.20
Swaziland	604.27
China	501.82
Cabo Verde	186.01
Macao, SAR China	162.43
Vietnam	158.89
Bhutan	132.35
India	126.69
Lao PDR	119.76
Sri Lanka	117.64
Korea, Rep.	101.35
Panama	90.45
Mozambique	74.76
Chile	72.92
Poland	71.83
Dominican Republic	71.45
Bangladesh	69.98

Table A. 8 (continued)

Country	*Change in Cg 2014/1990*
Mauritius	69.59
Albania	69.07
Malaysia	67.96
Singapore	66.50
Mongolia	62.59
Indonesia	60.71
Thailand	58.93
Ethiopia	58.79
Trinidad and Tobago	58.08
Peru	57.82
Lebanon	57.16
Belarus	55.32
Uganda	54.63
Armenia	50.43
Ireland	50.20
Botswana	49.87
Ghana	49.03
Uruguay	46.55
Guyana	46.50
Argentina	45.07
Azerbaijan	42.05
Burkina Faso	41.56
Hong Kong, SAR China	41.00
Tunisia	40.20
Chad	39.43
Lesotho	38.66
Costa Rica	35.35
Liberia	34.64
Nigeria	33.89
Nepal	32.21
Morocco	31.73
Israel	31.56
Kazakhstan	31.29
Egypt, Arab Rep.	29.72
Angola	29.06
St. Vincent and the Grenadines	29.03
Turkey	28.08
Turkmenistan	27.90
Seychelles	27.76
Uzbekistan	26.99
Sudan	26.28

(*continued*)

Table A. 8 (continued)

Country	*Change in Cg 2014/1990*
Rwanda	25.56
Malta	24.56
Bulgaria	24.44
El Salvador	23.69
Tanzania	21.44
Namibia	20.30
Phillipines	19.07
Bolivia	19.06
Iran, Islamic Rep.	18.49
Jordan	17.89
Romania	17.37
Zambia	17.23
Colombia	16.20
Pakistan	12.89
Papua New Guinea	12.85
Belize	12.61
Dominica	11.46
Tuvalu	10.55
Luxembourg	10.44
Grenada	10.25
St. Kitts and Nevis	10.01
Samoa	9.65
Nicaragua	9.44
Australia	9.34
Mali	8.76
Brazil	7.96
Norway	7.01
Cuba	6.59
Sierra Leone	6.29
Saudi Arabia	5.66
Suriname	5.13
Czech Republic	4.67
Malawi	4.12
Iceland	4.05
Ecuador	3.39
Sweden	3.11
United Kingdom	3.02
Austria	2.33
United States	1.77
Netherlands	0.73
Tonga	0.27
Germany	−0.12
Canada	−0.57

Table A. 8 (continued)

Country	*Change in Cg 2014/1990*
New Zealand	-1.00
Fiji	-1.74
Puerto Rico	-1.87
Guatemala	-2.23
Finland	-2.42
Paraguay	-2.84
Spain	-3.20
Mauritania	-3.92
Belgium	-3.93
Mexico	-4.34
Honduras	-4.85
Benin	-5.47
Algeria	-5.69
Denmark	-6.92
Portugal	-7.03
Marshall Islands	-8.56
France	-8.62
Iraq	-9.51
Bermuda	-10.06
Bahrain	-10.10
St. Lucia	-10.36
Russian Federation	-11.51
Cyprus	-11.61
Antigua and Barbuda	-12.09
Kiribati	-12.48
Japan	-12.73
South Africa	-13.09
Senegal	-14.03
Micronesia, Fed.Sts.	-14.92
Kenya	-15.44
Switzerland	-15.66
Greece	-15.91
Venezuela, RB	-17.05
Solomon Islands	-17.85
Congo, Rep.	-18.83
Vanuatu	-19.21
Andorra	-20.18
Oman	-20.27
Yemen, Rep.	-21.22
Italy	-22.14
Guinea	-24.33
Cote d'Ivoire	-25.61
Togo	-25.63

(*continued*)

Table A. 8 (continued)

Country	*Change in Cg 2014/1990*
Gambia, The	–25.74
Cameroon	–26.05
Niger	–27.74
Djibouti	–28.40
Barbados	–28.61
Brunei Darussalam	–32.15
Gabon	–33.00
Bahamas, The	–33.29
Comoros	–33.66
Kyrgyz Republic	–33.99
Georgia	–34.71
Guinea Bissau	–36.94
Madagascar	–40.27
Ukraine	–46.24
Moldova	–46.57
Burundi	–47.80
Zimbabwe	–49.31
Tajikistan	–49.59
Central African Republic	–55.64
Congo, Dem.Rep.	–56.22
United Arab Emirates	–61.84

Source: The author's calculation based on World Bank data.

Table A. 9 The national income coefficient (Cni): World in 1990

Country	*National income coefficient based on GNI PPP 1990*
1. Brunei Darussalam	9.863
2. Luxembourg	5.527
3. Switzerland	5.415
4. Bermuda	5.277
5. Macao, SAR China	5.163
6. Saudi Arabia	4.879
7. United States	4.699
8. Oman	4.373
9. Singapore	4.349
10. Iceland	4.167
11. Sweden	3.934

Table A. 9 (continued)

Country	*National income coefficient based on GNI PPP 1990*
12. Austria	3.873
13. Japan	3.833
14. Germany	3.831
15. Canada	3.821
16. Bahrain	3.794
17. Belgium	3.783
18. Netherlands	3.696
19. Denmark	3.624
20. Italy	3.576
21. Norway	3.515
22. France	3.488
23. Finland	3.484
24. Bahamas. The	3.484
25. Hong Kong, SAR China	3.356
26. Australia	3.302
27. United Kingdom	3.285
28. New Zealand	2.819
29. Spain	2.691
30. Greece	2.688
31. Israel	2.588
32. Ireland	2.462
33. Malta	2.327
34. Puerto Rico	2.285
35. Portugal	2.214
36. Gabon	2.214
37. Cyprus	2.007
38. Antigua and Barbuda	1.939
39. Venezuela. RB	1.830
40. St. Kitts and Nevis	1.787
41. Seychelles	1.743
42. Cuba	1.712
43. Barbados	1.682
44. Korea, Republic	1.668
45. Russian Federation	1.584
46. Iraq	1.449
47. Trinidad and Tobago	1.431
48. Ukraine	1.373
49. Suriname	1.329
50. Iran, Islamic Republic	1.302
51. Brazil	1.283

(*continued*)

Table A. 9 (continued)

Country	*National income coefficient based on GNI PPP 1990*
52. Malaysia	1.281
53. South Africa	1.276
54. Algeria	1.257
55. Uruguay	1.214
56. Lebanon	1.207
57. Mexico	1.147
58. Belarus	1.034
59. Macedonia, FYR	1.033
60. Georgia	1.026
61. Romania	1.023
62. Botswana	1.005
63. Bulgaria	0.985
64. Mauritius	0.960
65. St. Lucia	0.954
66. Colombia	0.941
67. Panama	0.908
68. Grenada	0.908
69. Costa Rica	0.906
70. Ecuador	0.889
71. Turkey	0.864
72. Jordan	0.857
73. Jamaica	0.856
74. Thailand	0.841
75. Dominica	0.834
76. Moldova	0.824
77. Chile	0.820
78. Fiji	0.771
79. Egypt, Arab Republic	0.751
80. Namibia	0.742
81. Tunisia	0.703
82. St. Vincent and the Grenadines	0.678
83. Peru	0.676
84. Guatemala	0.666
85. Belize	0.649
86. Dominican Republic	0.646
87. Mongolia	0.645
88. Congo, Republic	0.559
89. Indonesia	0.556
90. El Salvador	0.555
91. Albania	0.544
92. Phillipines	0.505
93. Morocco	0.498
94. Tonga	0.469

Table A. 9 (continued)

Country	*National income coefficient based on GNI PPP 1990*
95. Sri Lanka	0.467
96. Tajikistan	0.465
97. Armenia	0.461
98. Bolivia	0.455
99. Kyrgyz Republic	0.445
100. Yemen, Republic	0.438
101. Pakistan	0.395
102. Nicaragua	0.379
103. Honduras	0.376
104. Cote d'Ivoire	0.353
105. Nigeria	0.351
106. Cameroon	0.339
107. Mauritania	0.338
108. Vanuatu	0.334
109. Kiribati	0.315
110. Zimbabwe	0.314
111. Kenya	0.291
112. Zambia	0.282
113. Bhutan	0.280
114. Lesotho	0.277
115. Sudan	0.266
116. Guyana	0.258
117. Ghana	0.241
118. Senegal	0.230
119. India	0.224
120. Lao PDR	0.208
121. Cabo Verde	0.208
122. Madagascar	0.204
123. Papua New Guinea	0.198
124. Comoros	0.197
125. China	0.195
126. Guinea Bissau	0.192
127. Benin	0.183
128. Vietnam	0.180
129. Gambia, The	0.179
130. Tanzania	0.175
131. Togo	0.170
132. Bangladesh	0.166
133. Nepal	0.159
134. Solomon Islands	0.157
135. Sierra Leone	0.153
136. Congo, Dem. Republic	0.149

(*continued*)

Table A. 9 (continued)

Country	*National income coefficient based on GNI PPP 1990*
137. Mali	0.148
138. Equatorial Guinea	0.146
139. Chad	0.141
140. Guinea	0.136
141. Burundi	0.133
142. Central African Republic	0.119
143. Niger	0.116
144. Swaziland	0.109
145. Rwanda	0.109
146. Burkina Faso	0.105
147. Uganda	0.096
148. Ethiopia	0.083
149. Malawi	0.068
150. Mozambique	0.046

Source: The author's calculation based on World Bank data

Table A. 10 The national income coefficient (Cni): World in 2000

Country	*National income coefficient Cni – 2000*
1. Kuwait	9.214
2. Brunei Darussalam	7.741
3. Luxembourg	5.942
4. Singapore	5.340
5. United States	4.846
6. Switzerland	4.829
7. Norway	4.763
8. Bahrain	4.573
9. Oman	4.546
10. Macao. SAR China	4.234
11. Netherlands	4.218
12. Saudi Arabia	3.913
13. Sweden	3.855
14. Austria	3.840
15. Belgium	3.804
16. Denmark	3.799
17. Iceland	3.772
18. Canada	3.714
19. United Kingdom	3.626

Table A. 10 (continued)

Country	*National income coefficient Cni – 2000*
20. Hong Kong. SAR China	3.566
21. Italy	3.483
22. France	3.472
23. Germany	3.471
24. Finland	3.451
25. Japan	3.447
26. Ireland	3.387
27. Australia	3.361
28. Israel	2.977
29. Spain	2.859
30. New Zealand	2.662
31. Bahamas, The	2.640
32. Greece	2.518
33. Malta	2.439
34. Korea, Rep.	2.356
35. Slovenia	2.350
36. Portugal	2.297
37. Puerto Rico	2.268
38. Czech Republic	2.097
39. Antigua and Barbuda	1.886
40. Cyprus	1.829
41. St. Kitts and Nevis	1.826
42. Seychelles	1.824
43. Trinidad and Tobago	1.741
44. Gabon	1.546
45. Malaysia	1.543
46. Hungary	1.510
47. Venezuela, RB	1.486
48. Barbados	1.470
49. Slovak Republic	1.456
50. Croatia	1.423
51. Poland	1.403
52. Uruguay	1.336
53. Mexico	1.311
54. Lebanon	1.307
55. Palau	1.278
56. Iraq	1.246
57. Iran, Islamic Rep.	1.236
58. Estonia	1.226
59. Chile	1.223
60. Turkey	1.204

(*continued*)

Table A. 10 (continued)

Country	*National income coefficient Cni – 2000*
61. Mauritius	1.172
62. Cuba	1.148
63. Brazil	1.133
64. Lithuania	1.124
65. Latvia	1.070
66. Suriname	1.028
67. South Africa	1.008
68. Botswana	1.001
69. St. Lucia	0.987
70. Algeria	0.982
71. Panama	0.981
72. Thailand	0.946
73. Kazakhstan	0.940
74. Grenada	0.935
75. Costa Rica	0.916
76. Montenegro	0.911
77. Russian Federation	0.872
78. Colombia	0.856
79. Egypt, Arab Rep.	0.820
80. Jamaica	0.814
81. Bulgaria	0.812
82. Jordan	0.810
83. Equatorial Guinea	0.803
84. Dominican Republic	0.791
85. Macedonia, FYR	0.788
86. Tunisia	0.766
87. Serbia	0.758
88. Belarus	0.756
89. Fiji	0.749
90. St. Vincent and the Grenadines	0.747
91. Romania	0.746
92. Dominica	0.746
93. Swaziland	0.729
94. Ecuador	0.715
95. Belize	0.701
96. Peru	0.656
97. Guatemala	0.649
98. Namibia	0.641
99. El Salvador	0.639
100. Bosnia and Herzegovina	0.628
101. Indonesia	0.557

Table A. 10 (continued)

Country	*National income coefficient Cni – 2000*
102. Sri Lanka	0.556
103. Albania	0.546
104. Paraguay	0.542
105. Turkmenistan	0.523
106. Phillipines	0.517
107. West Bank and Gaza	0.489
108. Ukraine	0.485
109. Tonga	0.485
110. Mongolia	0.482
111. Morocco	0.462
112. Samoa	0.449
113. Guyana	0.440
114. Azerbaijan	0.439
115. Bolivia	0.438
116. Marshall Islands	0.416
117. Yemen, Rep.	0.384
118. Cabo Verde	0.382
119. China	0.378
120. Bhutan	0.374
121. Georgia	0.353
122. Honduras	0.351
123. Pakistan	0.346
124. Nicaragua	0.342
125. Congo, Rep.	0.340
126. Micronesia, Fed.Sts.	0.340
127. Armenia	0.312
128. Kiribati	0.304
129. Mauritania	0.288
130. Cote d'Ivoire	0.287
131. Vanuatu	0.279
132. Sudan	0.274
133. Vietnam	0.272
134. India	0.262
135. Nigeria	0.256
136. Uzbekistan	0.253
137. Zimbabwe	0.248
138. Moldova	0.246
139. Cameroon	0.234
140. Timor-Leste	0.234
141. Lao PDR	0.232
142. Ghana	0.229

(*continued*)

Table A. 10 (continued)

Country	*National income coefficient Cni – 2000*
143. Djibouti	0.226
144. Lesotho	0.223
145. Kenya	0.221
146. Zambia	0.219
147. Kyrgyz Republic	0.203
148. Senegal	0.196
149. Papua New Guinea	0.181
150. Solomon Islands	0.180
151. Bangladesh	0.175
152. Benin	0.170
153. Nepal	0.165
154. Gambia, The	0.156
155. Comoros	0.153
156. Eritrea	0.151
157. Tanzania	0.148
158. Madagascar	0.148
159. Cambodia	0.138
160. Mali	0.134
161. Guinea Bissau	0.134
162. Togo	0.133
163. Tajikistan	0.118
164. Guinea	0.116
165. Burkina Faso	0.108
166. Uganda	0.106
167. Chad	0.103
168. Sierra Leone	0.102
169. Central African Republic	0.087
170. Niger	0.080
171. Rwanda	0.079
172. Burundi	0.076
173. Liberia	0.070
174. Malawi	0.064
175. Ethiopia	0.064
176. Mozambique	0.056
177. Congo, Dem.Rep.	0.054

Source: The author's calculation based on World Bank data.

Table A. 11 The national income coefficient (Cni): World in 2014

Country	*National income coefficient Cni – 2014*
1. Qatar	8.750
2. Macao, SAR China	8.207
3. Kuwait	5.855
4. Singapore	5.455
5. Norway	4.562
6. Bermuda (2013)	4.524
7. Luxembourg	4.459
8. United Arab Emirates	4.428
9. Switzerland	4.020
10. Hong Kong, SAR China	3.845
11. United States	3.799
12. Saudi Arabia (2013)	3.587
13. Netherlands	3.323
14. Germany	3.229
15. Austria	3.225
16. Sweden	3.188
17. Denmark	3.183
18. Australia	3.035
19. Canada	3.015
20. Belgium	2.998
21. Ireland	2.913
22. Iceland (2013)	2.804
23. Finland	2.760
24. France	2.726
25. Oman	2.701
26. United Kingdom	2.687
27. Japan	2.591
28. Bahrain (2013)	2.571
29. New Zealand	2.461
30. Italy	2.388
31. Korea, Rep.	2.287
32. Spain	2.280
33. Israel	2.264
34. Trinidad and Tobago (2013)	2.190
35. Slovenia	2.063
36. Czech Republic	1.956
37. Portugal	1.929
38. Estonia	1.869
39. Slovak Republic	1.863
40. Malta (2013)	1.846
41. Greece (2013)	1.840

(*continued*)

Table A. 11 (continued)

Country	*National income coefficient Cni – 2014*
42. Lithuania	1.796
43. Seychelles	1.676
44. Malaysia	1.668
45. Poland	1.661
46. Puerto Rico (2013)	1.651
47. Hungary	1.629
48. Latvia	1.590
49. St. Kitts and Nevis	1.535
50. Russian Federation	1.530
51. Bahamas, The	1.515
52. Kazakhstan	1.476
53. Cyprus	1.469
54. Antigua and Barbuda	1.451
55. Chile	1.448
56. Croatia	1.422
57. Uruguay	1.374
58. Romania	1.356
59. Panama	1.334
60. Turkey	1.331
61. Equatorial Guinea	1.267
62. Mauritius	1.233
63. Lebanon	1.206
64. Belarus	1.197
65. Botswana	1.186
66. Venezuela, RB (2013)	1.180
67. Mexico	1.159
68. Gabon	1.153
69. Azerbaijan	1.150
70. Suriname	1.146
71. Bulgaria	1.144
72. Iran, Islamic Rep.(2013)	1.109
73. Libya	1.088
74. Brazil	1.080
75. Iraq	1.042
76. Montenegro	1.036
77. Thailand	1.018
78. Turkmenistan	0.987
79. Palau	0.974
80. Costa Rica	0.945
81. Algeria	0.920
82. China	0.895

Table A. 11 (continued)

Country	*National income coefficient Cni – 2014*
83. Serbia	0.886
84. Macedonia, FYR	0.881
85. South Africa	0.863
86. Colombia	0.857
87. Dominican Republic	0.846
88. Maldives	0.845
89. Jordan	0.810
90. Grenada	0.800
91. Peru	0.783
92. Mongolia	0.763
93. Ecuador	0.757
94. Egypt, Arab Rep.	0.750
95. Tunisia (2013)	0.749
96. Albania	0.746
97. St. Vincent and the Grenadines	0.731
98. Dominica	0.716
99. Bosnia and Herzegovina	0.715
100. St. Lucia	0.715
101. Sri Lanka	0.705
102. Indonesia	0.697
103. Namibia	0.682
104. Jamaica	0.587
105. Armenia	0.579
106. Fiji	0.571
107. Phillipines	0.569
108. Ukraine	0.549
109. Paraguay	0.545
110. Swaziland	0.536
111. Belize (2013)	0.522
112. El Salvador	0.521
113. Georgia	0.510
114. Morocco	0.510
115. Guatemala	0.497
116. Bhutan	0.494
117. Guyana (2013)	0.447
118. Cabo Verde	0.429
119. Bolivia	0.416
120. Uzbekistan	0.397
121. India	0.391
122. Nigeria	0.386
123. Samoa	0.381
124. Moldova	0.374
125. Vietnam	0.363

(*continued*)

Table A. 11 (continued)

Country	*National income coefficient Cni – 2014*
126. Tuvalu	0.360
127. Tonga	0.357
128. Congo, Rep.	0.349
129. Timor-Leste	0.346
130. Pakistan	0.345
131. West Bank and Gaza	0.340
132. Lao PDR	0.333
133. Marshall Islands	0.319
134. Nicaragua	0.317
135. Honduras	0.300
136. Sudan	0.271
137. Ghana	0.269
138. Zambia	0.262
139. Yemen, Rep. (2013)	0.254
140. Mauritania	0.251
141. Micronesia, Fed.Sts.	0.244
142. Kiribati	0.241
143. Bangladesh	0.227
144. Cote d'Ivoire	0.227
145. Kyrgyz Republic	0.219
146. Lesotho	0.215
147. Cambodia	0.208
148. Vanuatu	0.207
149. Sao Tome and Principe	0.201
150. Cameroon	0.200
151. Kenya	0.197
152. Papua New Guinea	0.189
153. Tajikistan	0.179
154. Tanzania	0.169
155. Nepal	0.164
156. Senegal	0.158
157. Chad	0.145
158. Afghanistan	0.137
159. Solomon Islands	0.137
160. Benin	0.137
161. South Sudan	0.124
162. Sierra Leone	0.123
163. Haiti	0.119
164. Zimbabwe	0.117
165. Uganda	0.114
166. Mali	0.111
167. Burkina Faso	0.110
168. Gambia. The	0.108

Table A. 11 (continued)

Country	*National income coefficient Cni – 2014*
169. Rwanda	0.104
170. Ethiopia	0.102
171. Comoros	0.099
172. Guinea Bissau	0.097
173. Madagascar	0.095
174. Togo	0.089
175. Guinea	0.078
176. Mozambique	0.078
177. Niger	0.064
178. Burundi	0.054
179. Malawi	0.053
180. Congo, Dem.Rep.	0.048
181. Liberia	0.047
182. Central African Republic	0.041

Source: The author's calculation based on World Bank data.

Index

F. Čaušević, *A Study into Financial Globalization, Economic Growth and (In)Equality*, DOI 10.1007/978-3-319-51403-1

The manufacturer's authorised representative in the EU is Springer
Nature Customer Service Centre GmbH, Europaplatz 3, 69115 Heidelberg,
Germany. If you have any concerns regarding our products, please
contact ProductSafety@springernature.com

Printed and bound by CPI Group (UK) Ltd, Croydon, CR0 4YY
30/09/2026
02225565-0001